Gaston Remembers

Produced in cooperation with the
Gaston Chamber of Commerce
and
Community Communications
Montgomery, Alabama

Gaston Remembers

Weaving a Tapestry in Time

By Sally Griffin

Corporate Profiles By Sheri Sellmeyer
Photo Editor Jim Brown, Jr.

GASTONIA
TROOP № 3
BOY SCOUTS
JUNE 4ᵗʰ 1917

BACK ROW, READING LEFT TO RIGHT: SCOUTS SLOAN, SMITH, JOHNSON, ZIMMERMAN, RATCHFORD, DEAL, WALKER, D., QUICKLE, FAYSSOUX, POSTON, & W.L. BALTHIS OF LOCAL SCOUT COUNCIL;
FRONT ROW: SCOUTS MORRIS, DENT, WALKER E., FERGUSON, TALLEY, SPENCER L., GRIER, MANGUM, BABINGTON, AND SCOUTMASTER R.K. BABINGTON.
SEATED IN FRONT: SCOUTS DAVIS AND SPENCER M.L.

$\mathcal{F}$oreword

$\mathcal{O}$n behalf of the Chamber of Commerce Board of Directors I am pleased to present to you *Gaston Remembers: Weaving a Tapestry in Time.* What better title could describe a rich heritage founded in textiles that has made us the leading manufacturing community in North Carolina today.

Since Gaston County was settled by the Scotch-Irish and German settlers migrating south from Pennsylvania in search of abundant water and fertile farm land in the 1750s, the ability of our people to adapt and innovate, along with a strong work ethic, is what has made us the pacesetting community of today.

Today, Gaston County continues to weave its future through expansions of existing manufacturers, attracting new industry, and encouraging the entrepreneurial spirit of a strong work force. Gaston County, the second largest in population in the Charlotte-Gastonia-Rock Hill MSA, is playing a leading role in the rapid expansion of one of the fastest growth areas in the United States.

From rolling hills to sharp jutting peaks reaching to the skies, Gaston County beckons those who love the gentle southern hospitality of its citizens. It beckons those who have the pioneer spirit seeking new opportunities to build a better tomorrow for their families.

The Gaston Chamber of Commerce is pleased to publish this book and hopes that it will provide a glimpse at what makes our community unique for those who live, work, and visit here. Our unique tapestry will continue to be woven by the people of Gaston County, to whom we dedicate this book.

Tim R. Helms
President
Gaston Chamber of Commerce

$\mathcal{P}$reface

$\mathcal{G}$aston County is rich in history and rich in memory. The ties that bind families trail through the centuries, thick at times with details and at other times thin, almost threadbare. Collecting the pieces of the county and trying to fit them together has been a task that at all times was rewarding, sometimes difficult, and most times enjoyable.

I could never have completed the work had it not been for a number of people and organizations who gave so much of their time and help. For nearly 20 years, I have collected interviews and personal pieces of information from those whose families settled this rich region, and I am grateful to every one of them.

The staff at the Gaston County Public Library spent enormous amounts of time running through files, checking and comparing data, and searching for more data. They watched with me through the windows in the North Carolina Room as the seasons changed and imagined what the first settlers thought as they watched the seasons change. Mary Ann Goodman was always there, ready to teach me once again about the microfilm machine, which I have yet to master, as well as to suggest yet another source for a tricky piece of information.

Steve Watts at the Schiele Museum gave me advice, directed me to books, and listened patiently to my manuscript for accuracy checks. I do not want to forget to thank Tim Cassell, Hunter Huss librarian, who scrounged through endless volumes to find and share rare books.

My friend Linda Roberts has read my manuscripts, offered suggestions and encouragement, all with a good dose of humor that I often needed.

Sheriff Leroy Russell has spent a good many hours over the years telling stories of the early growth of Gastonia and Stanley. And Alan Waufle of the Gaston County Museum provided me with a copy of the transcript of Caroline Shipp's trial as well as other historical facts during the years that I have known him.

I owe a great debt to Brenda Penley Hewes who has spent two years telling me about her childhood in Gaston County and plied me with numerous histories, papers, and other such treasures. She also believed in me and encouraged me when I thought the task was too great.

I also wish to thank Howell Stroupe whose stories have educated and entertained me since 1978. Howell has done much to preserve the history and the flavor of this county. Mrs. Ellen Shuford also offered advice, stories, and encouragement. She is a descendant of the founders of the county and has devoted a great deal of time to preserving the history.

Mildred Sadler is a pioneer and a wonderful example of courage who has told me many stories and whose stories I have used to encourage others. The same is true for T. Jeffers, deceased mayor of Gastonia, who always set high standards and was more than willing to share his knowledge of his town. And, of course, Dr. Ray Medford, who has spent his life collecting old farm machines, making them work again and displaying them. The fascination that Ray has for machines, iron furnaces, and the like is contagious.

It is to the storytellers that I am grateful—to everyone who ever called me to tell me a story about something in Gaston County. For it is they who started my collection of Gaston County facts and folk tales and who eventually brought about the writing of this book.

Sally Griffin

Community Communications-Book Division
Publishers: Ronald P. Beers, James E. Turner

Staff for *Gaston Remembers*
Publisher's Sales Associate: Fred Sommer
Executive Editor: James E. Turner
Managing Editor: Mary Shaw Hughes
Design Director: Camille Leonard
Designer: Samantha Woodham
Photo Editors: Mary Shaw Hughes
& Samantha Woodham
Editorial Assistant: Robyn Putz
Production Assistant: Corrine Cau
Proofreader: Opal Banish
Printing Production: Frank Rosenberg/GS America

Community Communications
A Division Of LWT Communications Inc.

James E. Turner, Chairman Of The Board
Ronald P. Beers, President
Daniel S. Chambliss, Vice President

*C*ontents

Getting Started: Who Settled the Area?

1

❏ *This replica of a Catawba Indian hut can be seen at the Schiele Museum's stockade. Photo by Jim Brown, Jr. #13*

❏ *Pen -and -ink drawing of a Cherokee Indian village by Chip Holton. Courtesy of Schiele Museum. #609*

*A*s is true for most of the land in the United States, the white man was not the first to put down stakes in what is now Gaston County. Long before the first white settlers arrived, a tribe of Indians known as the Catawbas had found the fertile land and ample rivers in the western part of what would become the Carolinas.

The Catawbas, a branch of the Sioux, had migrated from the Ohio Valley area and were living comfortably in what became the Carolinas, many historians believe, as long as 600 years before the first Conestoga wagon rolled down the trail. The Catawbas were industrious people who established a community in which they built huts, fished, trapped, hunted, and farmed.

But the Catawbas' territory of the lush forests and clean, sparkling streams and rivers also was claimed by another Indian tribe, the Cherokees, who were of Iroquoian descent and more warlike. The Catawbas and the Cherokees, whose mainstay was further west, fought over the land. Some accounts say that the Cherokees lost 1,100 men and the Catawbas lost 1,000 in the war. Whether or not the number of dead played into the final result is not known, but the Catawbas retained possession and the Cherokees retreated to the Broad River area, where they had lived before the skirmish.

Even as the Indians were settling the dispute over the ownership of the land, England's King Charles II was giving away the same land, and more, to eight of his friends, the Lords Proprietors. The land so generously given by the king covered most of what is now North and South

Carolina. In 1696, the British Crown had loosely claimed all the land that is now North Carolina, and the perimeters of what was to become Gaston County were located in the wide expanse of Clarendon County. As the number of settlers in the Carolinas increased so did the number of counties, a necessity because of the distance those who moved to the far outreaches of the territory had in traveling to the county seat to pay taxes, register deeds, and conduct other matters of public business. In 1729, New Hanover County emerged from Clarendon. Later, in 1734, Bladen County was formed, then Anson in 1749. The creation of more counties was a sign that more people were moving to the western areas of the territory—the population was increasing.

Most of those first white families who moved into what is now Gaston County came from Pennsylvania. A large number of Europeans immigrating to Pennsylvania had made land harder to find and more expensive. Expansive tracts of land in the west Carolinas were either free or could be purchased cheaply.

In 1701, an explorer, John Lawson, published a book relating his experiences in the untamed Carolinas. Whether the first settlers—the Germans, who were mistakenly called Dutch, the Scotch-Irish, and the English—learned about the area from reading Lawson's book or whether it was by word of mouth from people who traveled north on the old trading path to sell their goods and buy others is not known. However they heard about the territory, it sounded good to them so they loaded their belongings in wide Conestoga wagons, hitched up horses, mules, or oxen and headed south.

Among the first to brave the trail from Pennsylvania was Diedrich Ramsour. He came down the trail in the 1740s, selected a site about a half mile between the junction of Clark's Creek and another stream and set up a gristmill. Ramsour's Mill was built somewhere between 1745 and 1750 and was the first erected west of the main Catawba River. The site on which it was built remained in Lincoln County when Gaston became separate some 100 years later.

Ramsour was followed by Christian Reinhardt, who set up a tannery on the east bank of Clark's Creek.

By the end of the decade, enough people had tramped down the trail to establish a settlement near the present location of Lincolnton. These people, for the most part, got along with the Catawbas and the gentle Indians shared their land and their expertise with the settlers. Over time the friendship proved to be detrimental for the Catawbas because not only did the white settlers take their land, they brought with them the smallpox virus, which by 1759 had destroyed about half the Catawba tribe.

❏   *The most traveled routes taken by early settlers in their migration from Pennsylvania. Courtesy of N.C. Department of Archives and History. #36*

☐ *The paddle wheel and dam are all that is left of Ramsour's Mill, which was built between 1745 and 1750. Courtesy of Gaston County Art and History Museum. #533*

☐ *Courtesy of N.C. Department of Archives and History. #5*

The number of Indians continued to decrease as the number of whites increased, the whites claiming the fertile areas near the bountiful creeks and rivers to build their houses, marry, and raise their children.

In what later would become the eastern-most reaches of Gaston County, some Scotch-Irish, including the Leepers, McLeans, Dicksons, and Alexanders, built their houses and laid off their fields. Peter Eddleman settled in the north and set up shop as a cabinetmaker. Some of the finest pieces of furniture in these homes was made by Eddleman, and the settlers prized them.

Deeply religious, these Calvinists did not wait long after settling in to establish a meetinghouse. The story of the site selection for the church seems almost providential. A man passing through the area died and was

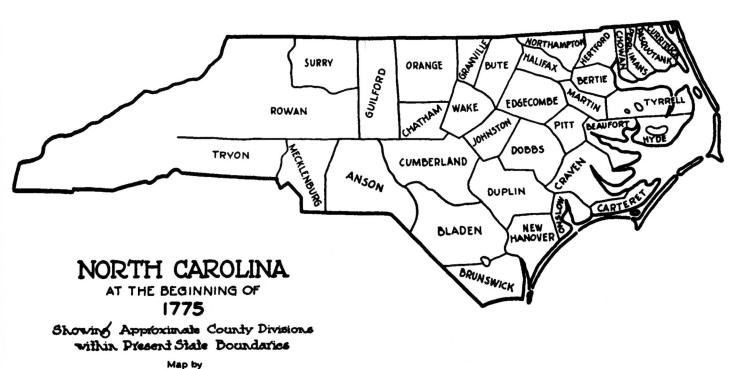

NORTH CAROLINA
AT THE BEGINNING OF
1775

Showing Approximate County Divisions within Present State Boundaries

Map by
L. Polk Denmark

buried in a clearing. Others who died were buried nearby. As the people began to visit the graves of their loved ones in this place in the woods, it took on a somewhat sacred air, and sometime before 1764, Elihu Spencer and Alexander McWhorter established a Presbyterian church on the spot. The fledgling house of worship, located in what is now North Belmont, was named Goshen. Humphrey Hunter, who arrived in 1795, was the first preacher at the log church. Hunter later helped establish a school.

Joseph Kuykendall, a German, unpacked his wagon and set up a home near the land settled by the Scotch-Irish. A creek in the area became known as Dutchman's Creek, apparently a reference to Kuykendall. Kuykendall and his family attended Goshen Church until Germans in a settlement near the present town of Dallas established a Lutheran church.

The Germans, many of whom came from Pennsylvania, migrated to North Carolina around 1740. Among the settlers were Peter Heyle, John Freitag, Bostian Bess, Adam Kastner, the Leyenbergers, Seigmunds, and Hochstetters. They were settling further north on the South Fork River near a creek that became Hoyle's Creek near what is now Dallas.

By 1750, when patents were registered for the land, the spelling of German names was anglicized—Hoyle, Friday, Best, Carpenter, Sigmon, Huffstetler.

Another settler in that area, John Sloan, found iron ore and built a smelting furnace to extract the ore. Sloan's furnace provided andirons, skillets, irons, and other domestic items for the settlers.

By 1767, the Lutherans had built a church on the South Fork near what is now Dallas. The church first was called Kastner's, after one of the first families, but the name later was changed to reflect a famous town in their native Pennsylvania—

❑ *This was the third building that housed the Pisgah ARP Church. Courtesy of Pisgah ARP Church. #336*

Philadelphia.

Another group settled on Long Creek, also near present-day Dallas. They, too, were Protestants, but their religion was Baptist. By 1772, they had built a log structure that was the first Long Creek Church.

Another group had settled near what is now Gastonia and had sprung from Goshen. Two more Presbyterian churches had organized. Near what is now Gastonia, Pisgah ARP Church branched off from Goshen; and Long Creek Presbyterian, near what is now Bessemer City. By 1795, New Hope and Olney Presbyterian Churches were in operation.

The land had been cleared, houses and outbuildings built, churches were going strong, and cemeteries had been walled in to provide a safe place for

Long Creek Presbyterian Church was organized near what is now Bessemer City. Courtesy of Long Creek Presbyterian Church. #131

the bodies of loved ones. All seemed well for most of the settlers in the new land.

This sense of happiness and well-being did not include business with George III, who became king of England in 1760, and William Tryon, whom King George had appointed governor of North Carolina. Where those two were concerned, the kindness of the settlers was wearing thin. It would not take much to push them over the edge.

The trouble that was brewing did not stop with England and her kings and governors. South Carolina's governor was stirring up the once-friendly and gentle Catawbas, encouraging them to raid the settlers' houses and

farms. The imaginary line that had been drawn between the two Carolinas was disputed and the governor wanted people who lived on land he claimed for South Carolina to pay taxes to him and not to the governor of North Carolina. The McLeans and others who had built their houses or cabins on land that formed a point between the Catawba River and the South Fork of the Catawba River decided to build a fort to protect themselves from the Indian raids. Using the rivers as barriers on two sides, the South Pointers stacked logs at the foot of a bluff and on the other open side, creating a fortress to protect them from the Indians or any others who might invade their settlement.

was put on his head, King George set up more tariffs and taxes for the colonists to pay. To add insult to injury, six years later Governor Tryon levied taxes to raise money to build himself a palace in New Bern, a town so far away from the Lincoln area that many of the people could only imagine what it was like or where it was.

In 1768, the people who had settled what would become Lincoln and later Gaston County were separated from Mecklenburg County into a county named after the hated governor, Tryon County—another source of aggravation. The governor's poll taxes in 1767 and 1768 had already made them angry, but having to live in a place that carried the name of the governor who lived far to the east and sent demands to the west was too much.

Court for Tryon County was held at the home of Christian Mauney, who set aside a room in his house to keep

the county records until a courthouse could be built. Mauney's house also served as the jail and the building in which all county business was conducted. A Tryon County courthouse was never to happen, though, because the disgruntled settlers already were getting ready to challenge the rule of England.

When the revolts became more open, Boston had its tea party and residents of Tryon County signed the Tryon Resolves, a demand for fair and equitable treatment that predates the U.S. Declaration of Independence.

Members of Tryon County formed safety committees. One such committee was formed in the eastern part of the county, headed by Colonel Joseph Dickson. Dickson also joined the Regulators, a group of men who later went to battle in South Carolina.

In 1776, with the Revolutionary War in full swing, Tryon County was dissolved and two new counties,

❏ *The Battle at Kings Mountain is credited as a major turning point of the Revolutionary War. Courtesy of N.C. Department of Archives and History. #32*

❏ *Goshen Presbyterian Church was reported as the oldest church in the county. Courtesy of Gaston County Art and History Museum. #28*

Lincoln and Rutherford, were formed. The town of Lincolnton was laid off. The boxes of records and the courthouse business for Lincoln County remained at Christian Mauney's house.

Dividing the counties and wiping Governor Tryon's name off the map was not enough for this brave and passionate band of people who had moved to the western section of Tryon County. Arguments grew more heated, the Crown's demands increased, and some settlers became more stubborn; the lines of allegiance soon began to form.

It was not long before the inevitable happened. War broke out, involving all 13 colonies and forcing the Indians to take sides. In Tryon County, the Cherokees took the side of the British and the Catawbas remained faithful to the patriots. Some of the black slaves, of whom there were few, fought alongside their owners, taking the same side the owners took.

Not all the white settlers took the side of the patriots. Some remained loyal to the British Crown. They preferred the stability of the Crown with its taxes and unfair demands to the unknowns of life under the patriots' government. They worried that if the patriots took over they would not have strong enough support to hold their government together. England's taxes were high and the demands were unreasonable, but they felt that was better than plowing into another unknown, even a possible anarchy. Some of those who took the side of the crown were Zachariah Spencer of Spencer's Mountain; a LaBoone of LaBoone's Mountain; and Lieutenant John Moore. Records indicate that the name John Moore was a popular one in Tryon County, so the Tory is identified as the son of Moses Moore. Another John Moore, the son of William Moore, was a patriot.

Also fighting with the British were the Hessians, mercenaries from the German province of Hesse who came to America for the sole purpose of fighting in a war.

As word spread that General Cornwallis was coming, the patriots and the Tories began to ready their arms. Colonel John Moore rode through the territory to encourage the Tories to save their crops for the winter to make sure that the British army had food.

The patriots also were getting ready. John Sloan changed the name of his iron works to Washington Forge, in honor of the famous general, and began making cannon balls. These three-pounders later were taken to Kings Mountain, but were not used because in the haste of battle, no cannons were taken to the mountain. In the eastern section, patriots gathered at the home of Joseph Dickson to practice military maneuvers and prepare for battle.

Also preparing for battle was

Colonel James Johnston, who lived near what is now Mount Holly, William Rankin, and Colonel Fredrick Hambright. Alexander Robinson, who lived near what is now Union Road in Gastonia, and his son James also readied to fight. James Robinson was a soldier in the battle at Kings Mountain.

Uniforms among the colonists were the same for both sides. Patriots and soldiers for the crown went to battle in the same shirts and pants that they wore to plow the fields and cut timber. William Ferguson, a Scotsman who fought for the British and was killed at Kings Mountain, is said to have worn a plaid shirt.

Three battles were fought in this area: at Cowan's Ford, at Ramsour's Mill, and at Kings Mountain.

It was at Kings Mountain, on

Col. William Ferguson was a Scotsman who fought for the British and was killed at Kings Mountain. Courtesy of U.S. Department of Interior-National Park Service. #532

October 7, 1781, that the South Fork boys, along with groups from Lincoln County, Rowan County, Tennessee, and other areas, charged the British. Some lost their lives, but the battle is credited as a major turning point of the war. Major William Chronicle, a 20-year-old who led a charge at the last minute when General William Graham left to attend to his sick wife, died when a musket ball struck his chest and exploded in his heart. Robert Henry, a young man at 15, was gored by a bayonet that went through his left hand and thigh. Henry survived this battle and killed his attacker.

Captain John Mattocks and John Boyd also died in the battle. Among those on the British side who were killed was Colonel Ferguson, who had worked so hard to organize the British soldiers and to prepare the troops for the coming of General Cornwallis.

After the local battles, many of the South Fork boys and the others went home to their wives and sweethearts. The dead were buried and the following spring the farmland was planted. For all but a few who continued the fight, meeting General Washington and fighting until the final cannon ball was fired, their part of the war was over.

John Sloan's Furnace turned from the manufacture of cannon balls to frying pans and plows. The name John Sloan does not recur in accounts after the war. However, the name Ormand does and the Ormand family history indicates that the Washington Furnace was on property owned by Ben Ormand, who received a land grant in 1754.

Just as Pennsylvania had become crowded in the first half of the century, the Carolinas experienced a population explosion in the second half. This took away the elbow room for some of the settlers, and they once again packed their wagons and headed for new territory—this time Tennessee.

General Joseph Dickson, who had fought so bravely at Kings Mountain, eventually left the county and went to Tennessee, but he remained until 1803 and served in the state legislature.

Robert Henry stayed for a while, surveyed land and helped establish a boundary between the two Carolinas before he, too, sought his fortune in Tennessee.❏

□ *Long Creek Presbyterian graveyard. Courtesy of Long Creek Presbyterian Church. #132*

2 *C*arving a County: Gaston Cuts Loose.

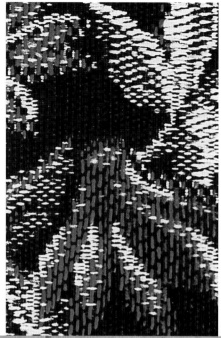

❑ *Thomas Rhyne was one of the first in the county to build his house of brick. Courtesy of Scott Lewis and the Rhynes. #44*

When the calendar pages turned to the end of the 18th century, the cannons and muskets of the Revolutionary War had been silent for 17 years; and Thomas Jefferson was in office—the third president of the still new United States. People in Lincoln County now were citizens of a fledgling new country with a democratic form of government. The first half of the new century passed in a flurry of activity. Farming remained a big chunk of the financial backbone of the county, but some of the crops changed. Virginians, who had depleted the nourishment of their land with too many tobacco crops, moved south looking for fertile land for another crop—cotton. Some of these people planted cotton seeds in the ground and their own roots in Lincoln County.

By 1810, cotton had become a major cash crop in the area. The cotton planters sought labor for the fields at the slave markets in South Carolina. In that year, 16,359 whites and 2,489 slaves lived in Lincoln County.

Blacksmith shops, forges, gristmills, and sawmills were springing up in every settlement and helping to create new settlements in what had been wilderness less than 100 years before. Tired of fighting, the people were ready to build houses, raise children, and increase their financial holdings—things they had wanted when they braved the trail to North Carolina half a century before.

Those who had acquired some land and some wealth in the years that they had been in Lincoln County built houses that were more than one-room cabins—many of those built in the first half of the 19th century resembled each other, however. They were one-and-a-half-story houses with one room on the first floor that doubled as bed-room and living room. The upstairs, in some cases not tall enough for an adult to stand in, had a bedroom and a storage room. The kitchen usually was in a separate building behind the house. The sawmills sculpted the raw logs into boards, which gave the houses a new look—clapboards to nail to the logs to give the houses a sleek look rather than the crude one of stacked logs chinked with mud.

Major Joseph Dickson and Colonel James Johnston had built their houses of brick, making the molds from wood, packing them with mud, and leaving them in the sun to dry. Dickson is believed to have built the first brick house in the county. Thomas Rhyne also built his house of brick and put the year it was built, 1799, in the side in a different color brick.

For some of those who had settled around the Catawba and South Fork Rivers, the fertile area had become too crowded.

As some moved out, others moved in. Two brothers, Jacob and Abraham Stowe, came from Virginia in 1810, bought property near what is now Belmont, and set out to farm and raise cotton.

Two other brothers, John and Jonas Hoffman, settled near Spencer Mountain and built gristmills along the river.

A populous area also suited John Fulenwider, who first came to Rowan County, fought in the battle of Ramsour's Mill, then moved to Lincoln County. He purchased land between Long Creek and Beaver Dam near High Shoals, built a smelting furnace, and began to separate the ore from the dirt and rock to get the pig iron needed to make domestic items for the kitchen and the farm. Fulenwider used a recently discovered

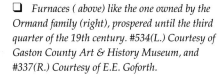

❏ *Furnaces (above) like the one owned by the Ormand family (right), prospered until the third quarter of the 19th century. #534(L.) Courtesy of Gaston County Art & History Museum, and #337(R.) Courtesy of E.E. Goforth.*

❏ *High Shoals Iron Works was a profitable business established by John Fulenwider. Courtesy of Observer Printing Co. and Wilma Long. #135*

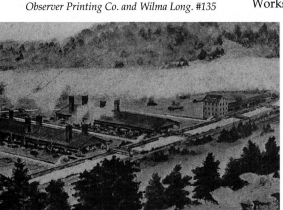

charcoal method to heat his furnace. He cut trees from his own forests and burned them to make the charcoal. The energy of the water from the shoals was used to generate the power to operate the bellows. By 1804, the Switzerland native had a profitable business, which he called High Shoals Iron Works. As had John Sloan in the Revolutionary War, Fulenwider had to change from the manufacture of domestic items to wartime items—cannon and shot—when England again invaded the United States in 1812.

Not far from the High Shoals Iron Works was Sloan's Washington Furnace, now Ben Ormand's furnace, which was turning out items from fire backs to irons and plows—peaceful domestic items the settlers needed. These furnaces prospered until the third quarter of the century.

Fulenwider found that, in addition to the rich red iron ore, his property had a more precious metal—gold. A vein of gold ran from Kings Mountain in the south to Pasour Mountain in the northwest. Gold also was discovered along the South Fork and Catawba Rivers on the east side of what would become Gaston County. The fever hit the Lincoln County area in the 1820s. In 1829, the gold that lay in the creases of Kings Mountain was discovered, and William Wilson formed a company with nine other men to dig the precious metal out of the mountain. By the time the mine ceased operations in the 1860s, more than $60,000 worth of gold had been pulled from the craggy mountains and hills. The Carter Hill Gold Mine was set up on Pasour Mountain. Others speculated on flecks of gold, bought land around Crowders Mountain, and sunk their picks and their hopes deep in the rock in search of the big vein. But all that glittered was not good quality gold and when Dr. Elisha Mitchell came from Chapel Hill in 1827 to look at the gold mines and visit with some of the entrepreneurs, he remarked in his journal that the gold from a Mr. Boggs' mine was mica. However, he allowed as how other mines in the area were producing a rather fine specimen of the precious metal.

All the glitter might not be gold, but it had some value and that meant there would be more ways of making a living than working a farm. The county was rich in mica, gold, iron, lime, and other metals and minerals that could be extracted and sold.

Much to the chagrin of many a traveling preacher, the good folks found more to do with the crops that were grown than simply canning, drying, and eating. The water that was so plentiful could be added to apples and corn to cook up a mash that when fermented made fine brandy and whiskey, respectively. The abundance of water, the rich soil, and relatively long growing season, coupled with the accessibility of the trade route, made the Gaston/Lincoln area a natural for the manufacture of liquor. At one time, more than 40 stills were registered in Gaston County. Toward the end of the 19th century, liquor advertising was as abundant as the alcohol consumption.

Taverns sprang up around the Belmont area and near the point where the South Fork joined the Catawba

River. Somewhere in this area the Hankses lived. Dick Hanks apparently was not one of the wealthy landowners, and his cabin was crude and small. Legend has it that his niece Nancy came to the area from Kentucky, moved in with him, and may have worked in a tavern near Belmont. A monument is located in the vicinity she is believed to have lived. Thomas Lincoln, whose family also had moved to Kentucky, returned for a visit and courted Nancy Hanks. They were married when Nancy became pregnant. According to the legend, the baby born to the young couple was to be president of the United States during one of the country's most trying times. His parents named him Abraham.

If the liquor stills were growing, so were the churches. The dust had hardly settled on the wagons of the first arrivals when the Presbyterians, Lutherans, and Baptists had cut down trees, shaped the logs, and built churches. The Methodists came to the Stanley Creek area in the 1840s and built a campground.

An Italian, Chevalier Riva de Finola, searched for gold in the eastern part of the county near Tuckaseege Ford.

Typical sawmill operation of the late 1800s and early 1900s. Courtesy of N.C. Department of Archives and History. #38

This plaque marks the site of Dicky Hank's log cabin. Courtesy of Gaston County Art & History Museum. #115

❑ *(top) Many speculated on gold and sank their hopes in the search for "the big vein." #31*
❑ *(bottom) Typical North Carolina gristmill. #30*
Photos courtesy of N.C. Department of Archives and History.

Workers in de Finola's mine were predominantly Irish and their religion was Catholic. For a while they worshipped in de Finola's home, but their dream was to have a church.

Hearing of their desires, a Catholic farmer, William Lonegan, who also wished to have a church of his denomination, donated land on Mountain Island, west of the Catawba, three miles from Mount Holly on Mountain Island Road, for the construction of a chapel. The chapel still stands, a monument of faith, on the island. The simple white frame building was built in the same style as many of those churches built in the mid-1800s. On each side of the center door was a window with shutters to protect the panes of glass when no one was inside the church. A tiny porch stretched across the front of the structure, mirroring the popular architecture of the period. It was a peaceful setting with the woods around the building and the water lapping softly on the shore. Construction on the building began in 1842 and was completed two years later. Judge William Gaston, who lived in eastern North Carolina and died in 1844, sent money to help with the cost of construction. Gaston was a devout Catholic who had been influenced by his mother, a woman who worked diligently to perpetuate the Catholic religion in North Carolina. Given the name St. Joseph's, the church prospered and by 1869 was well established. It remained the worship place for the county's Catholics until Belmont Abbey was built later in the century.

The growing population wanted churches for its soul and schools for its children. By 1823, the private Catawba School had opened near Tuckaseege Ford. And in 1826, M. O'Reilly opened an academy near Beatty's Ford. School was not held many months of the year and was more for those who had money than for the masses. The people of the small settlements of Garibaldi and Woodlawn wanted their children to learn at least the basics: reading, writing, and ciphering. Some of them would hire a teacher to come and work with their children, holding school in their homes or allowing the teacher to stay in their homes.

The rivers that had provided water and sustenance since the arrival of the first pioneer also provided a method to ship goods out of the county and bring other goods in. Boat travel up and down the rivers to Virginia and South Carolina increased with the demand to move goods.

Land travel on the Great Trade Route also increased. The rides were lengthy and uncomfortable on the backs of horses or on bumpy wagons and stagecoaches. Travelers needed rest and food, and horses needed the same. Folks who owned houses along the stagecoach route used part of their houses for rest stops and post offices. Travelers on the stagecoach, who were going to York and Lincolnton on the old post road or trail, often refreshed themselves at the home of John Falls. William Joseph Wilson, in the Crowders Creek area, also allowed his home to be used as a rest stop. Wilson was register of deeds in Lincoln County from 1799 to 1846, and his house was used as a post office as well as a stopping place for the stagecoach. Other houses on the stagecoach route included Peter Hoyle's house near Dallas. Hoyle's house, which was the post office when the settlement was called Hoylesville, had a window between rooms so the mail could be handed to people. Thomas Rhyne's

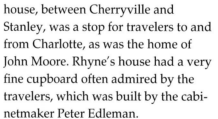

St. Joseph's was the only place of worship for the county's Catholics until Belmont Abbey was built later in the 19th century. Courtesy of Gaston County Art & History Museum. #60

At one point in time, more than 40 stills were registered in Gaston County. Courtesy of N.C. Department of Archives and History. #37

house, between Cherryville and Stanley, was a stop for travelers to and from Charlotte, as was the home of John Moore. Rhyne's house had a very fine cupboard often admired by the travelers, which was built by the cabinetmaker Peter Edleman.

Peace was not to reign in the county after the Revolutionary War or the War of 1812. Arguments were brewing over how the county should be divided and politics were hot and heavy. The lower end of the county wanted to be separated from the upper end, but the powers could not agree on where the line should be drawn. In 1845, Larkin Stowe, son of Jacob Stowe who lived near what is now Belmont, was elected to the state Senate. James Hillhouse White from the Crowders Creek area was elected to the House of Commons. These two men went to the state legislature with the purpose of making the area in which they lived a county separate from Lincoln County. With the help of Richard Rankin, from the eastern section of what would be Gaston County, they won. On December 5, 1846, a new county was born, cut from the southeastern part of Lincoln County.

What should they name it? Some of the names of the first settlers went through the legislature—Robinson, Alexander, and the like—but they were turned down.

A decision was made to name it for a judge, William Gaston, who was born in New Bern and had spent his life in the eastern part of the state. This was the same William Gaston who had donated money for the construction of St. Joseph's Catholic Church and who had died two years before Gaston became a county. At the same time, the center of the county was decided and named Dallas after the vice president of the United States, George Miflin Dallas.

The home of Jesse Holland was established as the courthouse and center of county business until such could be built. Holland sold the new county 75 acres for the new county seat.

When Stowe, White, and Rankin returned to their homes at Christmas, the year 1846 was drawing to a close, but it would be remembered as a mammoth one in the history of Gaston County. It is the year that the county broke away from Lincoln and became a county; Thomas Tate brought the first textile mill to the county; Belmont Academy opened. Progress was everywhere and things were looking good for those people who had made the decision to move south, and for their descendants.❏

❏ *Judge William Gaston, for whom the county was named, died two years before Gaston became a county. Courtesy of N.C. Department of Archives and History. #39*

*B*uilding An Industry: Rivers Aid Textiles

3

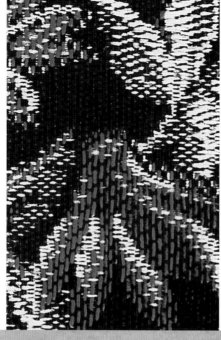

❑ *The Mountain Island Mill was established the same year that Gaston became a county. Courtesy of Gaston County Art & History Museum. #108*

*T*he Fulenwiders and the Ormands had iron furnaces; the Wilsons and the Fulenwiders, among others, had gold mines. James Henderson had built a gristmill three stories high which he had willed to Adam Springs. Other fledgling businesses were flourishing in brand-new Gaston County. The industry that would outlast the gold mines, remain when the iron forges were rusty and the gristmills had turned to dust, was textiles.

The first textile mill came the same year Gaston became a county and, like the first settlers, it came on a wagon from the north—northern North Carolina. Thomas Randolph Tate bought property on Mountain Island and set up a mill. He called it appropriately the Mountain Island Mill. Tate had bought the Mount Heccla Mill in Greensboro from Henry Humphreys, his father-in-law, who built the mill in 1828. As fuel became scarce, Tate first moved the building to a location near a major water source, then to Mountain Island where water from the Catawba River produced steam to power the machinery. The mill had looms and spindles—a spinning and

weaving operation for cotton and wool cloth.

The Mountain Island Mill rose four stories high out of the ground near the river. It was built of red bricks purchased from Mountain Island Manufacturing Company, which made them from the red clay. Construction was completed and the machinery was in place by the fall of 1848, when the machines began to hum and the first bolts of cloth rolled out of the mill.

In 1852, about six years after the Mountain Island Mill began operation, John Lineberger, Caleb Lineberger, Labon Lineberger, Jonas Hoffman, John Clemmer, and Moses Rhyne opened the Woodlawn Company below Spencer's Mountain on the South Fork near what is now McAdenville. Some accounts say that the machinery for this mill was ordered from England in 1840, which would make the Woodlawn older than the Mountain Island Mill. But other accounts give the year that operation began as 1852. The machinery was ordered from England, shipped to Charleston, South Carolina, then

❏ *The Woodlawn Mill (in the inset) was an imposing three-story structure with a basement and an attic. Lawrence Mill is pictured on the left. Courtesy of Archie & Anne Lineberger and Family. #744*

❑ *Spindles, shuttles, and bobbins are the typical tools of the textile industry. #661(L.) photo by Jim Brown Jr., and #222(R.) Courtesy of Dixie Yarns, Inc.*

❑ *There was plenty of business to go around, and the High Shoals Mill, like other mills and factories, was growing. Courtesy of Gaston County Art & History Museum and Mrs. H.C. Munga. #81*

☐ *McAden Cotton Mill #2 is a good example of the structural design of the times. Courtesy of Gaston County Art & History Museum. #49*

☐ *Slaves used large bags to collect and weigh cotton in the fields. Courtesy of Gaston County Art & History Museum. #51*

stone, and made their own brick. They also hired an engineer and dammed the river to get the water power necessary to run the mill. The finished mill was three stories high and had a basement and an attic. It was a spinning operation only.

An interesting story goes with the Woodlawn Mill. It is said that a number of young women were hired to work at the Woodlawn and that in the hours when they were off work they would go to the river and fish, using bent pins for fish hooks. Young men looking for dates would visit these women and coined the nickname Pinhook Girls from their fishing hooks. The mill took on the same name and, although it ceased operation years ago, it still today is sometimes referred to as the Pinhook Mill. Whatever name it is called, the mill operated for a number of years, spinning fine cotton yarn.

In 1846, Larkin Stowe and his sons, Jasper, W.A., and Edward B., bought 86 acres of land on the South Fork

brought to Gaston County part of the way by railroad and the rest of the way by wagon because the rails did not stretch to Gaston County.

Like the Mountain Island Mill, the Woodlawn was an imposing structure on land that had been virgin forest before construction began. The partners in this mill cut the timber, built kilns to season it, quarried their own

Caleb John Lineberger owned and operated several mills in the Gaston County area. Courtesy of John Caleb Steele. #747

❑ Caleb Lineberger raised capital using this ad in northern newspapers. Courtesy of A.C. Lineberger Family. #743

❏ *George Ragan sits at his desk at the Arlington Mill, which he built in 1900. Courtesy of Mrs. R.B. Babington, Jr. (Helen Howe) #383*

from George L. Ford and built Stowe's Factory between the site of the Woodlawn Mill and what is now Cramerton. The third mill to start operations in Gaston County, the Stowe Factory became operational sometime in 1853. This mill, built on the South Fork River, manufactured spun yarn. It was about the same size as the Woodlawn and had been built of materials found on the site, timber and red clay molded into brick. It took the Stowes three years to build the mill and more time to install the machinery.

Larkin Stowe was the son of Jacob Stowe who came with his brother from Virginia in 1810 to raise cotton.

The idea of building the mills began in the heads of these textile pioneers at about the same time, but each one operated a different timetable for getting his company into operation. Tate had the advantage of already owning the machinery and had only to move it

from one town in the state to another. The other two companies required time to decide what to purchase, then make the actual purchase and wait for the machinery to arrive.

It seemed that nothing could stop the progress in Gaston County. The Fulenwiders were hiring at the High Shoals Iron Works. Women and young girls were getting jobs in the mills. There was plenty of business to go around, land was still relatively cheap, towns were springing up, factories were growing, people were moving in, stores were opening. Life was good.

Although it seemed that Gaston was bursting at the seams with commerce, those first three textile mills in Gaston County would remain the only ones until the 1870s when the industry began to boom. Construction of new factories in the textile industry's infancy was curbed when the shots of the Civil War sounded, grinding most everything in the South to a halt and forcing the three mills already located in Gaston County to begin producing goods for the newly formed army of the Confederate States of America.❏

❏ *The Arlington Mill is the oldest in the Textiles, Inc. family of mills. Courtesy of Gaston County Art & History Museum. #349*

The War Divides the Country.

❏ *Mount Holly's first school was a typical one-room schoolhouse. Courtesy of Mrs. Thomas Worthy Springs, Jr. #572*

Prosperity was in the air for the area that took the name of Gaston. There was no doubt about it. A state public school law passed in 1839 mandated that children go to school three or four months of a year and gave twice the amount in state funds to counties that taxed its residents $20 for schools. Gaston was able to take advantage of this the day it became a county.

But the desire for their children to learn was as important to the people of Gaston County as the money they could get from the state. Schools sprang up in many communities, many of them with interesting stories. In 1830, land donated by Valentine Costner, near where Antioch Lutheran Church stands today, proved too difficult to get water to, so members of the community put the school on logs and rolled it across the road to land donated by Peter Costner, Valentine's son.

Another legend tells of a schoolhouse built on the Olney Church property. Parents and church members disagreed about whether it should be at the road or back from the road. The story goes that the schoolhouse was built away from the road. But the group that wanted it near the road went one night and sawed the schoolhouse in half, moving their half to the road. Later the two halves were put back together, but they never fit properly.

❏ *The original Gaston County courthouse was located in Dallas and later moved to Gastonia. Haithcox Photography #751*

Throughout the county, classes often were held in the winter when the children's labor was not as greatly needed as at planting, cultivating, and harvest times. Still the schooling was progress. The children were in buildings designated for school—mostly cabins with a hinged log in one side, or at the back to let in light, and a single door—and they were learning to read and write and to decipher a little math.

In many communities, one or two families built schools on their land and allowed the children who lived nearby to attend. Teachers were often preachers in the community or nearby. Sometimes they were from somewhere else, and in those cases they boarded with various families during the school term, staying with each family an average time of one week.

The factories did not yet pepper the landscape, but what were there, were doing well. High Shoals Iron Works, chartered in 1839, was turning out domestic items that sold nearly as quickly as they were turned out of their molds.

The new county seat was becoming a real town. In 1847, court was held in the home of Jesse Holland, but money was being raised to build a real courthouse. The 75 acres on the court square were stepped off, surveyed, and some offered for sale for homes, hotels, stores, and other businesses that would be needed by people visiting the county seat.

Laborers and slaves molded red clay into bricks and dried them in the sun to build the courthouse that was finished by 1848.

Slave labor also was used to make, stack, and mortar bricks into a jail. The jail was located on the court square and was a short walk from the court-

❑ *The life to which people in Gaston County had become accustomed would soon be gone. Courtesy of Gaston County of Art & History Museum. #345*

house, which stood in the middle of the square. It also was finished and ready for prisoners in 1848.

Conducting business at the court-house could take several days, and transportation from outlying parts of the county was not fast enough to allow many residents the luxury of going home at night and returning the next day. Those having business with the court often found that they would need a place to stay the night or the week.

John Smith had rooms in the Smith House, also known as the Farmers' Hotel, ready for rent when the first court session was held in 1848. A year later, the Matthews House was in business. The Pegram Hotel also was located in Dallas, as well as a tavern built by Nathaniel Hoyle, son of the Revolutionary War hero Peter Hoyle.

In 1852, Daniel Hoffman invited visitors to stay in his new three-story brick hotel across the street from the courthouse. Hoffman and his family lived on the third floor and rented out rooms on the second floor. On the first floor were parlors, dining rooms, and so on.

The great iron horse extended its tracks from Charlotte to Gaston County in 1860, coming first to Woodlawn Station, an area that later would be called Mount Holly. Before the end of the year, the tracks of the Seaboard Airline Railroad snaked through the woods to a community that railroad executives called Brevard Station. It was not happenstance that the station built at the end of the line was named Brevard. Robert Brevard had deeded more than 100 acres of land to the railroad with the under-standing that the station would bear his name. Later the name would change to Stanley Creek, from which the town of Stanley evolved.

Wagons or horses were available at the station for passengers whose desti-nations were farther west than the tracks traveled. The railroad was extended to Cherryville in 1862, dur-ing the heat of the Civil War.

It was for sure that the scars of the Revolutionary War were disappearing, replaced by dreams of prosperity. The people were beginning to forget the hard times and to look to the future and the good times. But that euphoria was not to last. Nor would the way of life that this corner of the South enjoyed.

Already rumors were circulating that slavery soon would be a thing of the past—the life that people in Gaston County and the rest of the South had begun to take for granted soon would be gone.

Gaston County would not be as hard-hit as some of the areas in the eastern part of North Carolina because its major agricultural product was food, not cotton, and the average size of the farms in the county was under 150 acres, unlike the thousands of acres that comprised the cotton estates in the east.

It also was talked that some of the residents of southern states wanted to pull out of the Union and form their own country to preserve their agrarian, sometimes decadent, lifestyle.

When these secession ideas first began to evolve in Gaston County, many of the people opposed them. Their grandfathers and fathers had fought too hard to establish the Union for them to be a part of breaking it up. Others took a pioneer spirit of not being told what to do and wanted to get yet another government off their backs.

Gaston County voters went with the majority of the people in the state when a referendum was held in 1860,

helping to soundly defeat a movement for this member of the original thirteen colonies to secede from the Union.

But in 1861, when Abraham Lincoln, president of the United States, wrote to the governor of North Carolina and asked him to provide a regiment for the Union army, the decision was reconsidered. While they were not in favor of seceding from the Union, they also were not in favor of fighting their brothers in the rest of the Southern states, especially when it meant fighting for ideas and a way of life their hearts were not in. That was not the way their fathers and grandfathers had decided to fight in the Revolutionary War. Their ancestors

❏ *People who had business to conduct at the courthouse often rented rooms in local homes or hotels like the Hoffman House. Courtesy of Gaston County Art and History Museum. #147*

❏ *William Groves Morris was a member of the "Gaston Blues Company" that was formed in Gaston County to fight the Yankees. Courtesy of N.C. Department of Archives and History. #617*

had been true to their beliefs and had stood up for them. It would have to be that way again. The people of Gaston would rekindle that independent spirit and fight for the beliefs held deep in their consciences.

Apparently others in the state were having second thoughts, for in May 1861, the North Carolina legislature voted to leave the Union and join the Confederate States of America. North Carolina was the last state to secede from the Union. The governor agreed to muster troops for the new country. Estimates of the number of men from Gaston County who heeded the call to arms range from 1,000 to 1,500.

In the Revolutionary War, the men living in the eastern part of the county along the South Fork River who joined the fight were known as the South Fork Boys. In the Civil War, they became the South Fork Farmers, organized by Thomas H. Edwards who was the regiment's captain. Samuel Stowe was the first lieutenant.

Another company formed in Gaston County to fight the Yankees was the Gaston Blues, organized by William Rankin, a descendant of soldiers who had fought in the American Revolution. Other officers in this company were William Groves Morris, first lieutenant, and George Hanks and Henry Fite, second lieutenants. This regiment was formed in the fall of 1861.

By 1862, Charles Q. Petty had organized yet another company from Gaston County.

Gaston County regiments followed the fight into the North, bravely standing their ground. At most of the major battles, as well as smaller skirmishes, names from Gaston County can be heard. They were far from their homes, their wives, their farms or fledgling stores and businesses. It didn't seem fair that they should have to fight another war, not even after so much blood was spilled on American ground in the Revolutionary War.

One of those who had to leave his home was Dr. Ephraim Holland, son of Jesse Holland. In 1857, Ephraim graduated from National Medical College in Washington, D.C., and returned to Dallas where he would practice medicine for 40 years. But his family practice was interrupted by the War Between the States, and he joined up to become the surgeon general of the North Carolina troops.

Industry rallied around the cause, with the High Shoals Iron Works putting domestic items on hold to make ammunition for the Confederacy. The Pinhook Mill turned its spindles and clacked its looms to spin thread and weave cloth to make uniforms for the men in gray. The mint at Charlotte became the headquarters for the manufacture of Confederate money, and gold from Gaston County probably became part of that money.

The first shot was fired in South Carolina at Fort Sumter in April 1861. It was not long after that first shot and the ensuing battle before the whole South was embroiled in the war. Gaston County, tucked into the base of the Appalachian and Blue Ridge mountains, was not safe from the Yankees and its soil again would be stained with blood, although not as much, just as it had been in the last century during the Revolutionary War.

Some residents of Gaston County opposed the war and formed the Peace Society.

William Wilson had died of a heart attack in 1854, and his brothers had left the county to go north and work with the underground railroad, a passageway for slaves to make it to the North to freedom.

The underground railroad was more active in Guilford County among the Quakers than in Gaston County, however.

Stories about the Civil War abound in Gaston County. One local legend has it that in his fiery march through the South, General Sherman went through some territory that was dangerously close to, if not in, the outskirts of Stanley Creek.

The winds of war did not bode well for the South. Gaston County, as did other areas of the South, had to put up with its share of deserters and looters who stole from their fellow Southerners, taking anything of value they could find.

But there was some profit for Gaston and its residents, too. The mills that manufactured cloth for the soldiers' uniforms for a while were paid from the coffers of the Confederate States of America.

War did not stop the great railroad from winding its way across Gaston County. Despite the fact that many of Gaston's sons were at war, the Seaboard Airline Railroad was extended to Cherryville in 1862.

There were some losses, too. Some of the county's sons fell in the bloody battles that pitted brother against brother.

The war lingered on for four long years, bringing devastation to much of the South. Mothers, sisters, and wives of the men from Gaston who had taken their muskets to Virginia, Pennsylvania, and other areas to defend their new country worked in the mills and with the slaves to cultivate the crops.

Each year the Town of Dallas recreates a Civil War battle. Whether there actually was a battle in Dallas is up for debate. However, we do know that federal troops arrived in 1865 to occupy the town after the war was over. General Robert E. Lee surrendered to General Ulysses Grant at Appomattox, Virginia, in April, but other generals surrendered later and federal troops were sent to numerous towns and cities to secure the area until all troops had surrendered.

Union troops were sent to Dallas because it was the center of a county from which troops and supplies were sent by railroad. We know that some skirmishes arose from the close contact of two opposing sides. During the war, Confederate soldiers had camped out and probably practiced maneuvers at the Brevard Station while waiting for the next train on which they would ship out. Gaston had become a major transportation point, and it was to the Union's advantage to shut that supply off. Lee might have surrendered to Grant a few weeks earlier, but it was necessary for the Union to quell all the

❑ *Dr. Ephraim Holland became the surgeon general of the North Carolina troups. Printed by permission of Ellen Holland Shuford. #111*

❑ *Confederate War Veterans' fife and drum corp. Courtesy of Dixie Yarns, Inc. #411*

❑ *It took more than a decade for Gaston County to recover financially from the war. Courtesy of N.C. Department of Archives and History. #608*

little skirmishes and battalions along the way to end the war.

Another Gaston County war legend says that during the occupation of the federal troops, John Campo, a Union soldier from Wisconsin, was patrolling the streets of Dallas one day when he saw some shoes in a local store window. He went in and stole the shoes, putting them on his battle-weary feet.

Campo was arrested, ordered to serve a jail sentence and to help carve the steps to the courthouse from granite. Following the popular architectural style of the time, two sets of steps wound to a common landing outside the courthouse's third floor, making it necessary to carve double the amount of steps needed to take a visitor to the courtrooms. The Union soldiers left the town before Campo's sentence was completed. But by the time Campo was free to go, he had come to like the town so he settled in Dallas and went to work for the quarry.

Gaston County's economic picture was not devastated by the freeing of the slaves, who had comprised a ready labor force, as were the cotton-producing counties in the east. But the county still suffered financially.

Farms did not produce at full capacity and industrial growth was quashed. It would take more than a decade for the industrial growth that showed such promise before the war to get back on track. The residents also had to address the needs of their new citizens, the freed slaves. Schools would have to be built for them, and jobs would have to be found. Labor that had been free after the purchase price of a slave was paid now would have to be paid on a per-use basis. Times had indeed changed.❑

❑ *Each year the Town of Dallas recreates a Civil War battle. Courtesy of 49th Regiment of the N.C. Re-enactment Unit. #653*

*P*utting it All Back Together.

5

❏ *The people of Gaston County began putting their personal and financial lives back together. Courtesy of Wilma Long. #192*

❑ *Accessibility to the rails was a necessity for the progress of an area. Courtesy of Mrs. Thomas Worthy Springs, Jr. and Observer Printing Co. #588*

*T*he war had taken its toll on the citizens of Gaston County. Hundreds were listed as dead or wounded. Among the numbers of the dead were attached last names of families that had been in the county for years—Fite, Armstrong, Costner, Craig, Paysour, Rhyne, Stowe, Rankin, White, Roberts, Skidmore, to name a few.

Others were captured and ill treated or were injured. They walked back to their hometowns or communities to continue the lives with their families that had been interrupted by the war.

By the end of 1865, the country had taken the renegade states back into the fold—was mending its rift, healing its wounds, and the county of Gaston needed to do the same. It now made sense for businesses interrupted by the outbreak of war to resume operations. Mills that wove cloth for the uniforms of the Confederacy had lost money in the last years because of the devastating condition of the fledgling country that would not survive. It was time to recoup those losses. Also, many would-be entrepreneurs who had visions of owning mills a decade ago still wanted to build mills. Those who

had farms wanted to raise crops and make a profit. The slaves are said to have stayed until the crops were in that fall. This year, though, they were paid wages for their labor, either in lodging, food, or in a few cases, money.

One business that would not survive the Reconstruction period was the High Shoals Iron Works. It had struggled under a new owner but was ready to fold. The fire that had puffed smoke into the atmosphere almost since the first white settlers had arrived died, and the vines and underbrush began their work to cover up any evidence of the once-powerful belching furnace.

Railroad tracks that were laid before and during the first years of the war needed to be stretched to more communities to link the county with other counties and other places. Officials of the Seaboard Airline and the Piedmont and Northern railroads were anxious to oblige. More track meant more business for the railroad, and more business for the railroad in turn meant more business for the Gaston area. Accessibility to the rails was fast becoming necessary for the progress of any area.

Railroad right of way was purchased so track could be laid through a settlement that later would be called Lowell. By 1870, the track was laid and railroad officials named the stopping place Wright's Station, after William Wright who lived in the house nearest the station. Later, the Linebergers, who owned the Pinhook Mill, had the name changed to the same as the mill's. By 1879, J.R. Glenn had opened a store near the railway station, the mills were up and running, people in the settlement cast their eyes toward progress. A young man from

Cherryville received its name because of a planting of cherry trees along Old Post Road. Pictured above is the Cherryville Band. Courtesy of Howell Stroup. #699

Massachusetts arrived and helped lay off the area for a town. His name was Neal Dumont, son-in-law of Caleb Lineberger. Dumont helped select a name for the town, a name that would be impressive when they sought state approval for incorporation. The name selected was Lowell, the same as an industrial center in Dumont's native state.

As the railroad tracks began to criss-cross the county, industry in the form of mills and factories began to dot the terrain. Names that appeared on incorporation papers for many of the mills were the same names that had appeared throughout the county since its beginnings. Other names not as familiar to Gaston Countians would appear as the area grew. The addresses would represent the North as well as the South. Some addresses would be as close as the town next door, Charlotte.

Some of Cherryville's early beginnings can be traced to 1851, when

Henry Summit opened a store where Old Post Road and the road to Morganton intersected.

The store provided a landmark and a beginning point for other businesses that could provide services for customers at the store. The road was lined with white pines so the area first took the name White Pines, but a planting of cherry trees along fences on Old Post Road changed the name to Cherryville.

Five years after the war, brand-new railroad tracks blazed in the sun in woods near what is now Belmont. In 1870, John Garibaldi built a watertank to fill the trains' boilers. As was its custom, the railroad company named the tank after a person, this time Garibaldi after the Charlotte iron magnate.

Wherever a train stopped meant an opportunity for businesses. The watering hole for locomotives was no exception, and soon after it was constructed a village sprang up nearby. A boost for the fledgling town was a store opened by brothers R.L. and S.P Stowe. The village, of course, took the Garibaldi name, probably at the insistence of the railroad.

The hardworking Stowe brothers were proud of their accomplishments. Their father had returned from the war with nothing and had married his childhood sweetheart, wondering how he would make it. As luck would have it, a man with a farm and no children invited Stowe and his wife to come and live with him. In exchange for caring for him the rest of his days, this man, Samuel Ewing, would give Stowe his possessions.

Even though life in the county was getting back to normal, it was almost a decade after the war before another textile mill opened in Gaston County.

In 1874, brothers A.P. and D.E. Rhyne, in partnership with Ambrose Costner, opened the county's fourth mill, the Mount Holly Cotton Mills. The mill was the first for Mount Holly and is believed by some to have inspired the name of the town, which was incorporated 15 years later.

In 1889, the communities of Woodlawn and Tuckaseege became one town—Mount Holly. One legend is that the Rhyne brothers and Costner wanted the town to take the name of a town in New Jersey that had a cotton mill reputed to spin the finest yarn of any place in the United States. Because of the similarity of the initials of the two states, N.J. and N.C., Rhyne hoped that some of the orders for Mount Holly Mills in New Jersey might find their way to Mount Holly Mills in North Carolina. Whether or not this happened, Mount Holly Mills in North Carolina did spin yarn and did prosper. The Huntersville name that the area had in the early 1800s disappeared when the post office, kept by the Reverend Humphrey Hunter, changed its name to Woodlawn. The

name Tuckaseege still appears on the outskirts of Mount Holly on a road sign identifying a back route to Charlotte.

The prospering of Mount Holly Mills evidently inspired the Rhyne brothers, and they invested money in 1883 with T.A. Davis to build Tuckaseege Manufacturing Company.

The Rhynes would wait five more years before establishing Mount Holly Knitting Company. Other stockholders included R.E. Costner, J.A. Costner, T.F. Costner, and M.R. Dewstoe. Later they would reorganize this company and change its name to Albion Manufacturing Company.

While the Costners and Rhynes were organizing Mount Holly Spinning, J. Harvey Wilson and James Moore became partners in Spencer Mountain Mills. It is interesting to note that Wilson was from Charlotte and Moore was from Maine—a joining of southerner and northerner in a business venture, a healing of the rift. Wilson later bought out Moore's interest and became the sole owner.

Five years later, the Linebergers, Caleb J., John M., and Lewis, would join with Henry Setzer to incorporate the old Woodlawn Mill. Probably because the Linebergers outnumbered the other investors, the company became known as Lineberger Mills. It seems that the name Woodlawn had no sticking power. The first Woodlawn Mill was nicknamed Pinhook, the second took the name of its owners, and the town that had been Woodlawn would change its name as well.

The mills took some time to reorganize after the war, but once the trend got rolling, there was no stopping it. After the new Woodlawn came Spring Shoals Manufacturing Company

❏ *Stowe Mercantile in Belmont was the product of the hardworking Stowe brothers. Courtesy of Gaston County Art and History Museum. #375*

McAdenville was named for the founder of the Spring Shoals Manufacturing Company, R.Y. McAden. Courtesy of Pharr Yarns, Inc. #673

A.P. Rhyne was one of the owners of the county's fourth mill, the Mount Holly Cotton Mills. Courtesy of the City of Mt. Holly. #564

owned by R.Y. McAden and his sons B.F., Giles, George, and Henry. The company was incorporated the next year. George A. Gray became superintendent of the mill and would remain until he gained enough knowledge, money, and credit to form his own mill. In 1883, the town of McAdenville was incorporated by the state. Named for the mill's founders, the town never changed its name.

The name Spring Shoals derived from Adam Springs who was born in 1776, the same year as his country. Springs, a graduate of the University of North Carolina, died in 1843, and legends about him still exist. Some say he was buried standing up so he could look over his land or watch his fish traps. Another story alleges he is the father of Abraham Lincoln, having courted Nancy Hanks when she lived with her uncle, Dickie Hanks, near

❏ *Some say Adam Springs was buried standing up so he could oversee his land. Courtesy of Mrs. Thomas Worthy Springs, Jr. #579*

what would become Belmont.

The McAdens bought the Springs property in 1880 and set up a mill on part of it.

Two years later W.J. Hooper and his wife, Emily, and W.T. Jordan began operations of Hooper Manufacturing Company but changed the name a month later to Mountain Island Manufacturing Company. They had built their plant next door to the old mill of the same name and later would buy the old building—Gaston's first mill.

George A. Gray had his money and his partners six years after he went to work at Spring Shoals. He joined with J.D. Love, R.C.G. Love, L.L. Jenkins, T.W. Wilson, Robert H. Adams, and J.H. Craig to organize Gastonia Cotton Manufacturing Company in 1887.

Mills and factories weren't the only progressive things going on in Gaston County. People who weren't associated with industry had found support businesses or other methods of making money.

Distilleries increased in the years between 1860 and 1870. The land was good and the water was plentiful—two necessary factors for good corn whiskey. The farmers were quick to pick up the art of harvesting corn and preserving it as alcohol. In 1860, more than a dozen distillers were registered. By 1880, there were nearly 50.

Sulphur and other minerals that permeated the land also were in the water, another of Gaston's blessings. In 1880, Dr. F.M. Garrett was operat-

ing a health spa in the western section of the county near Crowder's Mountain. Called the All Healing Springs, the spa consisted of a hotel and various springs in which visitors could soak their weary and ailing bodies, sometimes receiving a miraculous cure and other times having to be satisfied simply with a week or weekend of relaxation.

Newspapers were coming to Gaston County, too. George W. Chalk started *The Gastonia Gazette* in 1880. Other people, E.M. Evans and R.M. Martin, had tried to start newspapers, *The Herald* and *The Enterprise*, respectively, but their efforts had failed. Chalk sold the paper to his editor, J.E. Page, in 1885. Three years later, Page sold it to J.T. Bigham.

Education became important, too.

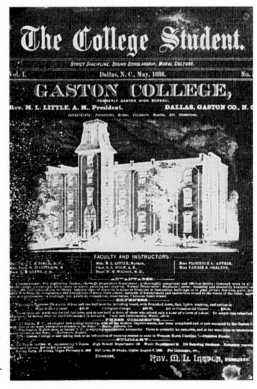

❏ *Courtesy of Gaston County School System. #582*

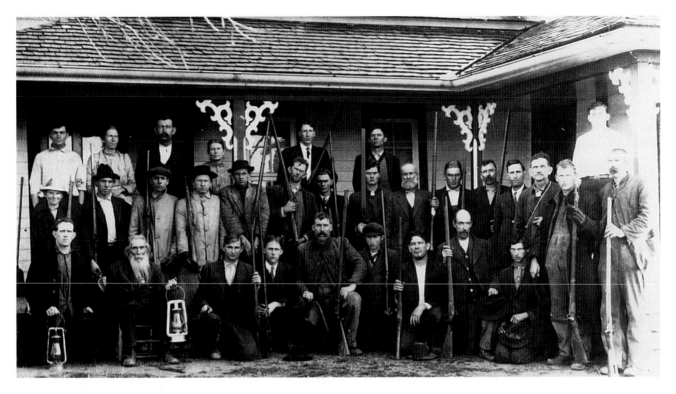

❏ *The Cherryville Shooters visited their neighbors' homes to "shoot in" the New Year and ensure prosperity. Courtesy of Fred and Creola Houser and Howell Stroup. #541*

❏ *(top left) The Oakland High School faculty taken in 1899. Courtesy of Charles Gray and the Gray Family. #625*

❏ *(bottom left) To build a strong economy, the community needed educated children. Courtesy of Gaston County School System. #560*

To build a strong economy would take educated children, and these citizens knew it. They began to build more schools.

Sometime around 1878, the people in Dallas organized a stock company and raised $1,500 to build a two-story, 30- by 50-foot building to replace a log structure that for years had been the home of Gaston Academy. When the building was completed the next year, the cost was $700 more than had been projected. The new building, on what is now South College Street, was called Gaston High School. Marcus Lafayette Little was the first principal, and girls and boys both were allowed to attend. Little spent his summers recruiting students for the fall classes. Students from grade school through college were invited to attend. At one time, girls from as many as six states attended the college, and a part of the school took the name of Gaston Female College and offered boarding facilities

for young women. The private school received some financial support from area Lutheran churches.

In 1886, the college portion of the school was named Gaston College.

Little was killed in 1891 in a train wreck near Newton. After his death, enrollment declined and in the spring of 1905, Corinne Puett walked across the stage and took her diploma—the last person to receive a diploma from the college.

Emily Pruden came to Gaston County from New England. Her mission was to establish a school for black girls. During her time here, the deaf woman established 15 schools. By 1890, boys were attending Miss Pruden's school and the name had been changed to Lincoln Academy, a boarding school for underprivileged children. Tuition and fees were a monthly rate of $4.50.

Since the war had ended and recovery had begun, the crops were

❏ *It was a time of great prosperity for many Gaston County residents. Photos courtesy of Jennie Craig Watson.*

543

#540

harvested, wood cut for fuel, people were looking for better times.

In the area around Summit's store, the descendants of the original German settlers cleaned their muskets and got ready to make their own kind of luck. As they had done every New Year's Eve, and as their fathers before them had done, these men gathered at one house, ate a hearty meal, and prepared to visit their neighbors' homes to shoot in the New Year.

Firing the muskets and chanting, drives away the witches and goblins and ensures a prosperous new year. The custom continues today and apparently is pretty effective. Cherryville is one of the most prosperous areas of Gaston County.□

558

*T*urning the Century.

6

❏ *The turn of the century brought good times to Gaston County. Courtesy of Wilma Long. #445*

❏ *Cherryville Manufacturing Company was the first mill in Cherryville. Courtesy of Howell Stroup. #704*

❏ *Martin Harry Shuford was the sheriff of Gaston County from 1891-1896. Printed by permission of Ellen Holland Shuford. #76*

*T*he last 20 years of the 19th century and the first 20 years of the 20th century marked tremendous growth for Gaston County. Mills hummed as they spun miles and miles of yarn destined for points throughout much of the United States and some foreign countries. The train whistle's wail and the great iron horse's wheels grinding the steel tracks became familiar, comfortable sounds. In churches, voices raised in songs of praise filled Sunday mornings and wafted out across the hills and valleys to reverberate the goodness of life throughout the county. Every day the hustle, bustle, and buzz of building, manufacturing, and business deals in the making seemed to be everywhere. Communities around the mills became towns. Some incorporated and grew into cities; some remained small and intimate, kept their community flavor, shunned the trappings of state sanction.

Cherryville traced its beginnings to a store at a crossroads. The first mill, Cherryville Manufacturing Company,

came in 1891, 10 years after the town was incorporated. More followed, including Nuway Spinning, Howell Manufacturing, Rhyne-Houser Manufacturing, and Carlton. Children grew quite well in the town of Cherryville and some received their education at Cherryville Academy, a school that was started in 1892 by about a half dozen citizens. The small frame building was located at the end of a street that later was named Academy Street. The first class—six young folks— graduated in 1911. Schools were important to Cherryville. Residents supplemented the money for four months of school that the state paid with the money for four more months of school.

Cherryville Manufacturing Company was started by John Rhodes, David Polycarp, David Mauney, John J. George, H.S. Sellers, P.M. Hauser, D.A. Rudisill, Lee Self, D.W. Aderholt, and S.S. Mauney. Cost of construction was $30,000.

The town of Garibaldi evolved around the Stowes' mills and the water tower that fed the trains that huffed and puffed from Charlotte across the rivers and through the woods and back again. Incorporated

❑ *Mount Holly became an incorporated town in 1889. Pictured here are Mount Holly's first firemen. Courtesy of the City of Mt. Holly. #570*

in 1895, its name was changed to Belmont, partly at the urging of officials at the newly opened Belmont Abbey College.

Mount Holly became an incorporated town in 1889, enfolding other little communities—Woodlawn, Tuckaseege—in its borders. Mills and their communities dotted the area long before the town got its name and received its incorporation papers from the state legislature.

Gastonia and Dallas, incorporated in 1877 and 1863 respectively, added people to their town limits at every census, but Gastonia's numbers were beginning to surpass those of Dallas. McAdenville attributes its name to the McAdens of Charlotte who had come to Gaston County to purchase and operate the mill that was started by Adam Springs. The name of Spring Shoals Manufacturing Company had been changed to McAden Mills.

Incorporated in 1883, the town was growing as the demands for yarn grew. The McAdens financed and

opened to the public a library, one of the finest in Gaston County. They studied and implemented other ways to increase the comforts and enjoyment of life for their employees.

J.H. Mayes bought the Holland farm in the early 1900s and built a mill, Mays Manufacturing Company, which was organized in 1906. The name changed to Cramerton Mills, Inc. in December 1922, but the town was not incorporated until 1967. Cramerton Junior High School retains over its front door its first name, the same as that of the first industrialist to come to the town—Mayworth School.

Cramerton oldtimers remember when Stuart Cramer, one of the original investors, assumed control of the mill and built his house at the end of a road that wound its way to the top of the mountain. Cramer donated food from his vegetable gardens to the school to help young women learn to cook, made cloth from the mill available for the school's sewing classes, and shared his radio with the townfolk

❑ *Stuart Cramer (above) was one of the original investors in the Mays Manufacturing Company. He built his estate (below) at the end of a road that wound its way to the top of the mountain. #727,(above) Courtesy of Mr. & Mrs. George B. Cramer and #478,(below) Courtesy of Jim Heracklis.*

on weekends. The hot days of summer sometimes were whiled away sitting on the dock of the railway station and listening to the announcer's voice on the radio recount the pitches, hits, and runs of baseball games. It was really something like a miracle, residents said, to hear those voices traveling across the airwaves.

J.P. Glenn built the first store in Lowell in the 1880s, after the railroad had bisected the town and success seemed imminent. The store had glass windows and enclosed the post office and a bar as well as daily items needed by the general population. Lowell was incorporated in 1889.

The Art Cloth Mill started in 1922. It was to be an innovative mill, making a decorative, tapestry-type cloth. The

owners of this mill had ideas that theirs would be the finest of all cloth. They imported workers and built a school for the children of the workers. In 1903, Dogwood College opened and the town seemed on the way to success.

The fancy new mill was destined to fail. Not enough demand for the cloth, a coming depression, and an inability to find enough skilled workers spelled the demise of the innovative industry. A.C. Lineberger later took over operation of the mill, changing its name to National Weaving Company. Lowell Cotton Mills and Peerless, already established in Lowell when the Art Cloth rose up, continued to operate.

High Shoals, the site of a Catawba Indian village long before the white

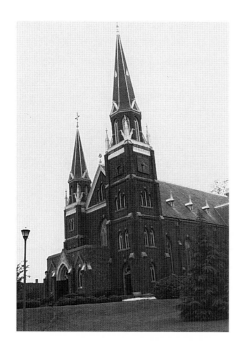

Belmont Abbey was originally named
Maryhelp Abbey. Photo by Jim Brown, Jr. #483

men came, became the site of the High Shoals Company. The list of owners includes D.A. Tompkins, Fred Oliver, and R.M. Miller, Jr.

At the top of a hill, the High Shoals Hotel, a clapboard dwelling-house-type structure, became a place of residence for the mill workers. Later it would become a residence for the superintendent of the mill and even later a mill office.

Dave Abernethy built a livery stable beside the railway station and had a thriving business delivering packages that came on the train as well as taking passengers where they wanted to go.

High Shoals, gateway to Lincoln County, had much more than a defunct forge and a new mill. The shoals themselves provided nature's background music and a beautiful spot for picnics. Many in Gaston County still recall the fun they had at church picnics or an afternoon spent wading the shoals with a favorite beau.

One of the first churches in High Shoals was St. John's Episcopal. In

1902, Eva Crump, of Texas, and Mary Neaves arrived to start an Episcopal mission. They taught music, art, nursing, and housework how-tos—all important things for young ladies to know. With all its amenities, the town chose not to incorporate until 1973.

Crowder's Mountain has drawn visitors for hundreds of years, and the fascination with the towering peak also was keen in the late 1800s and early 1900s. It was at the base of Crowder's Mountain that Dr. F.N. Garrett decided to construct a health spa. Garrett, of Kings Mountain, opened All Healing Springs in June 1881 and offered 50 acres of adjoining property to anyone who would open a private school for young ladies.

Emily Pruden, a deaf woman from Minnesota, took Garrett up on his offer. Later she deeded the school to the American Presbyterian Association. Through the years, its name changed from Jones Seminary to Linwood College.

Miss Pruden noticed, as she worked to get the school for young white

New schools sprang up all over the county as the population grew. Courtesy of Charles Wetzell. #371

ladies functioning, that the young black girls were more education-deprived than the young white girls. She established a school for them across the way, putting the educational facility in an old house. This was the beginning of Lincoln Academy, later to become Lincoln High School in Bessemer City.

Education of black children was lacking, but churches and other people set out to improve the situation. Pleasant Ridge AME Zion Church built a one-room log cabin school for black children on Spencer Avenue in the southwestern section of Gaston County. Later, three rooms had to be added to accommodate increased enrollment.

In 1890, black families in the Lowell area petitioned the Gaston County school system for a school for their children. Ten years later, in 1900, the county built a one-room school, Mountain School, which remained in service until 1960.

Higher education also was coming

to Gaston County. Monks from the Benedictine Order in Latrobe, Pennsylvania, came to Belmont after the Rev. Jeremiah O'Connell purchased the Caldwell farm and declared that a Catholic school would be built. The monks arrived in 1876, and classes started soon after with a handful of students. The school today would be classed as a high school and was called Maryhelp Abbey. Later, the academic work became more difficult, and the curriculum was changed from high school to college. The name Belmont Abbey was given to the school in 1913.

A group of nuns built just down the road from Belmont Abbey a college for young women. It opened in 1887 under the name Sacred Heart. The Sisters of Mercy also founded an orphanage, Saint Ann's, on the grounds. The orphanage later was closed.

In Gastonia, members of Main Street Methodist Church saw the need for a church-supported high school in their town. Oliver W. Davis donated land at the corner of Oakland and Elm Street (later called Second Avenue), and George A. Gray contributed heavily to the construction of the school. Professor Benjamin E. Atkins of Tennessee had connections with the Methodist church and was hired as headmaster. Atkins came to Gastonia in 1896, and Oakland High School opened with 84 students. Atkins

☐ Churches and other people set out to improve the education of the black children. Courtesy of Howell Stroup. #698

George A. Gray began his textile career as a millworker and moved from overseer and superintendent all the way to founder and stockholder. Courtesy of Gaston County Art & History Museum. #75

left two years later, and Professor Joseph H. Separk took the headmaster position. In 1901, the school became the first public school in Gastonia.

Schools were not the only items faced by the Methodist church and the residents of Gaston County. Liquor was a hotly debated issue. By 1880, Gaston County had 48 licensed liquor distilleries, many owned by prominent citizens. Gastonia allowed no drinking within its limits but did not prohibit the manufacture. State tax was a dollar a gallon, and many a gallon of liquor was shipped at night to avoid the tax.

Many members of the Methodist church and others wanted consumption of alcohol forbidden throughout the county. They were successful in getting a prohibition bill passed in the state legislature in 1891, but their euphoria was short-lived. The bill was repealed in 1893.

By 1890, Gaston County had a dozen or so textile mills. Population was increasing as people moved in to work in the mills. *The Gastonia Gazette* was publishing several times a week. Gaston County was becoming a hub for business and pleasure.

Bessemer City was incorporated in 1893, bringing the total number of incorporated towns in Gaston County to seven. Unlike many of Gaston's towns that fed on textile business, one of Bessemer City's first major industries was a lumber plant. The lush forests that surrounded the clearing that became Bessemer City made a lumber plant a natural for industry. Later another natural resource, clay, was extracted from the ground to make bricks, a second industry necessary to the building trade and in a sense to the textile industry, but not a part of textiles.

Reidsville tobacco industrialist John A. Smith came to Bessemer City in 1891 with his brother Turner and his wife's brother John Pinchback. He came with the intention of starting a town and that he did. He laid off the land into streets and avenues. The avenues were named after the states in the United States. The streets were numbered. City Hall and the opera house, as well as the jail and much of the business district, lined West Virginia Avenue.

Smith started a newspaper, *The Bessemer City Record*. The paper still exists; its editor, Lois Smith, has just announced her retirement. He also built a hotel on the side of Whetstone Mountain, expecting tourists and hoping to establish a mecca for them. That dream never materialized, and Smith later tore down the hotel and built himself a house.

Before the close of the 19th century, a young black woman from Gaston County became the last woman to be hanged in North Carolina. Caroline Shipp was sentenced to hang for the death of her 2-year-old child, and the deed was carried out on December 18, 1891. People from everywhere came to watch the woman die just as they had earlier that summer crowded into the courthouse to hear the testimony from the hired girl who had gone to a store and bought rat poison a short time before her child died.

W.W. Rutledge, formerly of the Philadelphia Church section of Dallas, said he was a youngster when Caroline Shipp was taken by wagon to the hanging tree near the old county home in Dallas. He said she sat on her coffin on a wagon and sang hymns as

□ *Caroline Shipp rode from the old Gaston jail in Dallas (above) to her death at the end of a rope. Haithcox Photography.#750*

Mr. John A. Smith, Founder of Bessemer City

□ *John Smith, a Reidsville tobacco industrialist, came to Bessemer City with the intention of starting a town. Courtesy of Bessemer City Record and Lois Smith. #748*

she rode from the jail in Dallas to her destiny with death.

Her executioners gave her a few minutes to say her last prayers after they placed the noose around her neck. The signal that she had finished her prayers was the white handkerchief in her hand. She dropped the handkerchief and the bottom dropped from under her feet.

The slender young black woman swung from the rope, but she did not die. Rutledge speculated that her swinging without dying was a sign of her innocence. But he said a deputy sheriff from Cherryville apparently did not think so. He grabbed her body and swung on it until her neck broke, Rutledge said.

The rope that choked her and finally broke her neck was cut into pieces and

handed out as souvenirs. Rutledge said he got a piece of the rope, but his father made him throw it down into the dust.

Her body was put into the pine box that was dropped in the ground a short distance away at Potter's Field. Sometime during the night she was buried, the body of Caroline Shipp was snatched from its grave. Legends say her skeleton later was found in the office of a local doctor. That is not as scandalous as it might seem. Robbing graves in paupers' cemeteries was commonplace throughout much of the United States in the late 19th century, because donations of bodies for study was not prevalent and grave-robbing afforded one way for doctors and would-be doctors to acquire cadavers for study.

Whether or not Shipp was guilty in the death of her child is up for questioning. Many believe her boyfriend, Mack Farrar, may have done the deed. Others say the child was not poisoned but died from dehydration brought on by a bout with a diarrhea and vomiting virus.

By 1911, Gaston County was dotted with textile mills and all indications were that more mills would be coming. Support industries, lumber mills, brick yards, and other businesses were increasing and doing quite well in the successful little county.

Brevard Station had changed its name to Stanley Creek earlier. By 1911, when the town sought incorporation, the Creek was dropped in favor of just plain Stanley, much to the chagrin of railroad officials who feared the town would be confused with the county of the same name but different spelling. Stanley had long been the stronghold of Methodists who, in the 1840s, built a campground near what would become the town. By the 1870s, Methodists from everywhere gathered at the old campground annually—

some more often—to renew their faith.

These dedicated Christians put up a school in 1903. Money came from the Methodist Conference, and the land was donated by W.D. Thompson and E.L. Pegram. Later the Methodists turned over the school to the county, and the site of the academy is now an obstacle course in front of the present Stanley Junior High School. The old building was torn down in 1919 and replaced by a brick building with an auditorium on the second floor.

Owners of the mills, interested in maintaining a big corner of the textile market, continued to experiment with new ideas. The first knitting operation came to Gaston County on February 6, 1888, when Abel P. Rhyne, J.A. Costner, R.E. Costner, T.F. Costner, and M.R. Dewstoe opened a small two-story mill. The mill was the third for Mount Holly and the ninth for Gaston County. A little more than a year later, in October 1889, the knitting machines were sold, and the mill switched to what a later generation would learn that Gaston County does best—spinning. This mill was operated by Abel Rhyne (who with his brother Daniel in 1874 had built the first mill in Mount Holly and the fourth in Gaston, the Mount Holly Cotton Mills).

Proudly and innovatively, the movers and shakers of Gaston County ushered their towns and communities into the 20th century. As the pages of the calendar indicated that another century had become history, Dallas remained the county seat, had three hotels, and Gastonia had 30 stores and factories and four cotton mills and two hotels. Oil lamps lighted the business district at night.

Gastonia began to eye the courthouse at Dallas, and the town's position as county seat as something it wanted. Town officials and businessmen made their bid to move the county seat to their town early in the 20th century and brought it to a vote. Twice the vote failed, but in 1909, the larger town prevailed and in 1911 the county seat was moved. County records were put into a new courthouse paid for in part by contributions from businessmen in Gastonia.

George A. Gray named himself president and John F. Love vice president on March 6, 1899, on a charter for Ozark Mills. Gray had begun his textile career as a worker in a mill and had worked hard through phases of mill operation. He had little formal schooling, but was an avid reader. He became an overseer, a superintendent, and finally attained the financial security and ability to move to the highest point—founder and stockholder of a mill.

What man could control seemed to be doing quite well. Mills opened and closed; people came and went; but success was prevalent, and the people of Gaston County seemed to be able to make the best of whatever came along.

Natural disasters, however, began to cause some setbacks. On August 31, 1886, an earthquake violently shook Charleston, South Carolina. The vibrations from that quake were felt in Gaston, rousting folks out of their beds in the middle of the night as the earth shook under their feet. The earthquake did not last long and did not leave any permanent irreparable damage. It did, however, bring to mind the ease with which things can be taken away no matter how careful man is.

Another disaster came on July 16, 1916, two days after an evil wind blew into the county, sending a cyclone through the area. The cyclone brought

❏ *The movers and shakers of Gaston County ushered new towns and communities into the 20th century. Courtesy of Jennie Craig Watson. #596*

GASTONIA
TROOP № 3
BOY SCOUTS
JUNE 4th 1917

BACK ROW, READING LEFT TO RIGHT: SCOUTS SLOAN, SMITH,
JOHNSON, ZIMMERMAN, RATCHFORD, BEAL, WALKER, D.,
QUICKLE, FAYSSOUX, POSTON, & W.L.BALTHIS OF LOCAL SCOUT
COUNCIL;
FRONT ROW: SCOUTS MORRIS, DENT, WALKER E., FERGUSON,
TALLEY, SPENCER L., GRIER, MANGUM, BABINGTON, AND
SCOUTMASTER R.K. BABINGTON.
SEATED IN FRONT: SCOUTS DAVIS AND SPENCER M.L.

❏ *The first Gaston County Boy Scout troup. Courtesy of Mrs. R.B. Babington, Jr. (Helen Howe). #63*

rain tumbling out of the pewter skies –rain that swelled the rivers that for so long had been Gaston's progress and success. This time the rivers worked against the people, overflowing their banks, sending muddy, swirling flood waters through the streets and homes. Stories of churches floating down the river, people jumping into the river to save Bibles and artifacts, and houses being pulled loose from their foundations to swirl around the waters and float downstream are told by some of the older residents, who still remember the day the rivers came into the streets.

Water levels inside houses were measured by mud rings around the ceilings of the first-floor rooms. For a

cyclone to blow inland was a strange occurrence, and for it to cause so much flooding and damage was even stranger.

Railroad tracks were washed away in parts of Gaston and Mecklenburg counties. A Southern Railroad employee, H.P. Griffin, was drowned. When the waters subsided, his body was found partially buried in sand and mud near the Belmont bridge where he had been working when the angry waters snatched him up and hurled him to his death. He was one of 19 workers who died in the flood.

As they had done in the past, residents of Gaston County assessed their damages and set out to repair and replace. Benefits were held to raise

money for the less-fortunate victims of the flood. Gaston County made arrangements to borrow money to replace the bridges and streets that were destroyed, and commissioners met with those of Mecklenburg County to discuss the repair of shared bridges and roads. Their spirits might be daunted from the recent disaster, but they were far from dead.❏

❏ *The Catawba River railroad trestle (above) being rebuilt after the flood of 1916. Courtesy of the City of Mt. Holly. #566*

❏ *Col. Armstrong (left) and his family were caught in the flood and could not get home. Courtesy of Charles Wetzell. #59*

Success Ends in Depression & Strike.

7

❑ *The promise of a job and a decent place to live brought in new residents by the hundreds. Courtesy of Gaston County Art and History Museum. #96*

*D*espite a few fires, an earthquake, and a flood, times were good in Gaston County.

Another town asked to be incorporated. It had no mills and was comprised of a very few families, but the Dellinger families wanted an identity. So it was that the legislature granted a charter to the town of Dellview in 1925. Gaston County now had 11 incorporated towns.

The mills ran so well that everybody who lived in the county and wanted a job could have one in the mill. Soon the workers could not meet the demands, and the owners had to seek workers from other areas. Their search took them to the mountain areas of North Carolina, other parts of the

state, and to Tennessee and Kentucky. The promise of a job and a decent place to live brought new residents by the hundreds. They came in wagons loaded with their belongings and settled into houses owned by the mill. They paid rent, bought on credit at the company store, went to church, and prayed that a better life was on the horizon.

The textile business flourished and houses of unbelievable size rose out of the red clay in Belmont and Gastonia as the mills made the owners rich.

Wealth was reflected in the fine clothes the folks wore and the motor cars they purchased. Gentlemen and ladies formed civic clubs to sponsor youth groups, aid the less fortunate,

❑ *The wealth of the mill owners was reflected in their clothing and their homes. Photo by Jim Brown, Jr. #1*

❏ *Mount Holly Main Street in 1928.*
Courtesy of Mrs. Thomas Worthy Springs,
Jr. #573

The workers often complained that their pay was too low, and the living conditions were poor. Courtesy of Fred Goodson. #128

and improve their county.

Theaters and opera houses flourished. Lush lawns, gardens, sun porches, and parties—all were a part of the 1920s in Gaston County. On the other side, the poor and the workers complained that their hours of work were too long, the pay was too low, and living conditions were squalid. The rosy life they had envisioned when they moved in and signed on had not materialized. They wanted some changes.

Despite the complaints of some of the workers, mill expansion continued, and the workers continued to show up when the whistle blew. The Grays and the Loves purchased land in Gastonia and began construction on what would be the world's largest mill under one roof. As late as the 1970s, the building still carried that reputation among the locals. Named Loray after the founding families, the mill was a fine brick structure with the latest equipment.

Arrangements to send the product manufactured at the mill to China were halted by the Boxer Rebellion.

The owners found that they had no other market for their goods and realized that they would lose a great deal of money through no fault of their own. In 1923, in an effort to recoup as much of their loss as possible, the Loray Mill was merged with a Rhode Island company, Manville-Jenckes, which also took over the operation of High Shoals Manufacturing Company.

Unrest continued among the workers. They continued to complain about hours and pay. The owners of the mills built more houses for the families, dormitories for unmarried workers, and established areas for recreation. In some cases, they contributed heavily to the construction of schools to educate the offspring of the workers.

It was too little too late, the workers said. They demanded to have higher wages. A high fence built around the Loray Mill particularly angered them, and they complained that not only were they underpaid, they now were locked in as if they were slaves or criminals. The fence was the last of a long line of insults, they said, and some of them quit their jobs. Undaunted, the mill owners replaced the workers with other workers.

The Gastonia Gazette printed stories implying that the mill strike was organized by Fred Beal of Massachusetts, the son of mill workers and said to have been a member of the Communist Party since 1928. Beal worked with George Pershing, who wrote for *The Daily Worker*, the newspaper of the Communist Party, to start a chapter of the National Textile Workers' Union in Gaston County. Their target was the Loray Mill. In March 1929, five mill workers were fired for causing trouble. On the first day of April, all the workers who were

❏ *The Loray Mill was the target of an organized strike in 1929. Courtesy of Gaston Chamber of Commerce. #314*

affiliated with the union walked off their jobs.

The mill was crippled by the striking workers, but the owners attempted to keep it running. The town talked of little else and the newspaper took the side of management. As tempers rose, Governor O. Max Gardner sent in the National Guard.

As talk of Communism continued, some of the workers returned to the mill. They said they did not agree with the Communist doctrine and would take their chances back at the mill. Others stayed out, holding out for better conditions and maybe a chance to have more voice in the day-to-day operation.

Beal held a meeting on June 7, 1929, at a site near the mill. In the crowd were curiosity seekers, dedicated Beal supporters, and some workers. Gastonia Police Chief O.F. Aderholt was killed during a gun battle between police and Beal's supporters

❏ *This picture of the strike organizers appeared in the* **Gazette** *before the strike and helped the police with correct identification. Compliments of* **The Gaston Gazette** *and the Gastonia City Police Department. #189*

Sixteen Gastonia Strikers and Organizers Charged With Murder, Defended by International Labor Defense
Loray Mill Strike

❏ *Gastonia Police Chief O.F. Aderholt was killed during a gun battle with the strikers. #54 (L.) courtesy of Gastonia City Police Department and #120 (R.) compliments of **The Gaston Gazette** and Charles Wetzell.*

as the strikers formed a march to the mill. Three policemen and a union member were injured.

The violence did not end there but festered until September 14, when mill worker Ella Mae Wiggins was shot and killed as she rode in the back of a truck to a demonstration site. Wiggins left a number of children whose support was what had driven her to complain and demonstrate for shorter hours and better pay. She also left a number of ballads about the strike, which she had written and sung.

Strike organizer Beal and his companions were convicted of second-degree murder. Before the appeal to the North Carolina Supreme Court could be heard, the men had escaped. It is widely believed that they went to Russia.

As if the bloodshed during the strike were not enough, the stock market took a giant leap downward in the fall of 1929, and many in Gaston County lost much or all of their holdings. Some found their heavily mortgaged homes no longer belonged to them, some were out of work, some had lost their businesses, and their savings. It seemed that dark despair would replace forever the euphoria of a few years before.

Again the spirit of Gaston County rose up and refused to be whipped in the face of trouble. We will rebuild, the leaders said. People will have to have clothes, the armies will have to have uniforms, parachutes, tents. The mills and their workers would make these things and get back to their prosperous positions.

Working together to bring back the times that they had became a way of life for the people of Gaston County. Times might be hard, but they had children who would live to see better times, and there was a need to band together and build for these children. It was during these times that people

THE GASTONIA POLICE DEPARTMENT IN 1925

from the communities took food to the school lunchrooms, built buildings with their hands, cleared the rocks and the clods of dirt to make playgrounds, planted shrubbery around the school buildings, and raised money from the pitiful pittances to be had for better schools.

The pioneer spirit of hard work and sacrifice stood the people of Gaston County well, and their strength helped pull them out of the depression and back onto solid footing.❏

❏ *Three Gastonia policemen and a union member were also injured in the strike. Gastonia Police Department pictured above. Courtesy of Dixie Yarns, Inc. #158*

❏ *A mill worker, after leaving a demonstration site, was shot at Gambel's crossing (bottom). Courtesy of Bill Phillips. #754*

Growing, Growing, Growing. The 1940s thru 1980s.

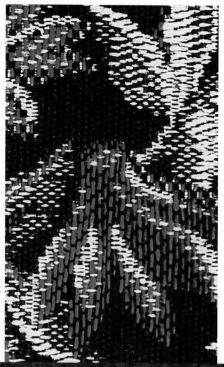

❑ *Sacred Heart College lost its financial battle, but its facilities have been put to use as a nursery for exceptional children and other community needs. Courtesy of Jim Heracklis. #480*

❏ *The North Carolina Orthopaedic Hospital was a godsend for crippled children all over the state. Courtesy of Gaston County Art and History Museum. #113*

❏ *Robert Babington, Sr. crusaded for a children's hospital for eight years. Courtesy of Gaston County Art and History Museum and Shelby Studio. #523*

*T*he years between 1940 and the present marked even more construction and growth.

The North Carolina Orthopaedic Hospital was built high on a hill on New Hope Road in Gastonia in 1921.

Robert Babington, Sr. fought for eight years to have a facility of that sort financed by the state. His faught began in 1909, and ended in 1917 when the state legislature approved the plan. At last Babington's dream would come to fruition.

The hospital proved to be a godsend during an epidemic of polio. Children who were afflicted with the dread disease were taken to the hospital for treatment. A March of Dimes official from New York said she remembered the height of the polio epidemic when the lawn of the hospital was white with tents. Parents were camping out to be as close as possible to their children who were fighting for their lives as the paralysis crept into their bodies, stopped their limbs from working, and squeezed the air from their lungs. In the 1950s when the vaccine was discovered and the polio dragon was whipped into his cave, the Orthopaedic Hospital did not close its doors. It became the salvation for crippled children all over

the state. Children with club feet, spina bifida, curvature of the spine, and other bone disorders received treatment at the hospital. Since the treatment could last for months, school was set up for these children, ensuring that their physical problems would not create educational ones.

The end of the 1970s brought the end of treatment of children at the orthopaedic hospital. The buildings were not abandoned; however, part of the operations of the county's department of social services has moved into the hospital buildings.

Taking care of the sick has always been a priority in Gaston County. From the earliest hospitals that were founded by Dr. Lucius N. Glenn, people have supported their local hospitals.

Other hospitals were Gastonia in the Highland section, Garrison on York Street, and the Negro Hospital on Marietta Street in Gastonia. In 1973, Gaston Memorial was built on a mountain overlooking Gastonia. Architect for the new hospital was Hugh White, Jr., son of the man by the same name who lived in a simple bungalow on Fourth Avenue in Gastonia, but put the flair into Gastonia's city hall and public library (now the home of the police department) and the elegance in the Gastonia High School building.

Also in this period, Sacred Heart College fought the declining enrollment with a night school program for older students, but lost the financial battle and closed. It was with a heavy heart that the people of Gaston County, many of whom had graduated from the school or had children who graduated from the school, watched the last day of class and viewed the empty campus that for so

❏ *1946 Veteran's Day Parade on Main Street in Gastonia. Courtesy of Jim Heracklis. #482*

❑ *The trolley made travel within the city easy.*
Courtesy of Robert "Ezra" Nolen. #602

❑ *Linwood Airport in 1941. Crowders Mountain in background. Courtesy of Jim Heracklis. #477*

❑ *Charter members of the Gaston Lifesaving Crew. Courtesy of Carol Brackett. #650*

❑ *Gastonia Old City Hospital later became Gaston Memorial Hospital. Courtesy of Scott Lewis. #67*

many years had vibrated with the voices of young women.

Sacred Heart students were invited to continue their education at Belmont Abbey as the community and the Sisters of Mercy pondered over what to do with the buildings that for so many years had been landmarks in Belmont.

Some of the buildings have been put to use as a battered spouse shelter. On another part of the campus, Holy Angels, a nursery for exceptional children, has grown from a tiny room in a house to a multimillion-dollar facility with a staff and plenty of love and special education for all the children who live there.

The beautiful Ashley High School was changed to a junior high school and Gastonia students were divided between two high schools, Hunter Huss and Ashbrook, creating a rivalry that has continued to fester for more than three decades.

A change in the educational system came in the mid-1960s when black and white schools were merged. Timidly, black students, a handful or less at a time, approached the formerly white campuses of Gaston's schools. Equally timidly, black teachers walked up the steps of white schools and put their

❑ *Gastonia High School (left) was later renamed Ashley High School for Principal Frank L. Ashley (above). #271(L.) Courtesy of Gaston Chamber of Commerce and #138(R.) courtesy of Dixie Yarns, Inc.*

Sacred Heart students were invited to continue their education at Belmont Abbey (above). Courtesy of Gaston Chamber of Commerce. #317

books on desks in rooms that would become theirs. Awkward at first, integration became a way of life with the students, teachers, and parents with few if any incidents.

Tight money in the 1970s contributed to the merger of the city schools in Cherryville and Gastonia with the county schools. W.P. Grier Junior High School was the last school built by the city of Gastonia, and it still had a new smell when it became part of the county system.

In 1964, Gaston College, part of the state community college system, opened its doors near Dallas. The Gaston Technical Institute became part of the college, which has enjoyed tremendous growth since its beginnings. The school now offers many majors, both in technical and academic areas. An arts program brings dancers, singers, and playmakers to the college's auditorium.

Another school, the North Carolina Vocational Textile School in Belmont, offers hands-on lessons in textiles to students from all over the state. The school works with other colleges to give students an opportunity for more than a technical degree.

The 1980s brought another change

in the liquor laws when the wet forces and the dry forces met at the polls after a hard-fought and bitter battle over whether liquor could be served by the drink in Gastonia. By a slim margin, the wet forces carried the vote and liquor-by-the-drink became a reality. During the same period of time, Cherryville approved a liquor store, becoming the third Gaston County town with ABC stores. The pendulum had swung the other way and the liquor that had been so prevalent in the county's early history returned, but control was tighter and the serving limited.

Like the century before, the 1980s marked a growth period for Gaston County. New industry moved in. Houses popped up all over the county. Industrial parks sprawl in all directions in many of the towns. Museums are preserving the county's past and are teaching the residents and visitors to appreciate the past and to use the past to make the future richer.❑

Gaston College is part of the state community college system. Haithcox Photography. #752

Getting Ready for the 21st Century.

❑ *Rendering of the proposed Civic Center for the Gaston community. Courtesy of the City of Gastonia.*

The Hoffman Hotel in Dallas has become the home of the Museum of Art and History. Courtesy of Gaston County Art and History Museum. #690

*A*s the 20th century passed the halfway mark, Gaston County began making preparations for the next century—determining the legacy it would leave its children, as their forefathers laid plans for what they would leave them. What would it be?

Governments and private groups formed task forces to evaluate the present, and ordered demographic and needs-assessment studies to get an idea of what should be done now to parade the county proudly into the next century.

A civic center—a place for activities. Charlotte, a major metropolitan area and as short a drive as 15 minutes from Gaston, has made itself a name in the stock car racing business, acquired an NBA team that went to the playoffs in the 1992-1993 season, and now is building a stadium for its newest acquisition, a national football team. There would be events that people from Gaston County would want to attend that would not have a place to be in Charlotte, and entertainment that would draw a smaller crowd would

not be feasible for such large spaces as Charlotte had built. Gastonia and Gaston County officials decided that the area needs its own civic center. Years of talking, planning, and surveying the public have resulted in a definite plan that is now in the works.

Renovation of old buildings and revitalization of neighborhoods are everywhere. In 1979, the Hoffman Hotel in Dallas became the home of the Museum of Art and History of Gaston County. An old homeplace, ghosts, and memories were preserved and opened for the enjoyment of the county. Since the hotel building received a new life, part of the grounds in the back have become the site for a new carriage house for the sleigh collection, one of the finest public collections anywhere.

The stately Ashley Junior High School, formerly Gastonia High School, whose main building was completed in 1927, has been renovated to luxury apartments, an attractive anchor to the York-Chester neighborhood. Many houses in the York Chester Historic District met the wrecking ball, but many others have been saved and are used as inns and offices as well as family dwellings. Young people with an eye to the preservation of the past are working to

The Cramer mansion on top of Cramer Mountain has become the anchor for Cramer Mountain Country Club. Photo by Jim Brown, Jr. #720

❑   *In 1973, Gaston Memorial Hospital
was built on a mountain overlooking
Gastonia. Photo courtesy of Gaston Health
Care.*

❑   *The main branch of the Gaston Public
Library is located on Garrison Boulevard.
Photo by Jim Brown, Jr. #721*

restore the neighborhood to its turn-of-the-century stature.

The Cramer mansion on top of Cramer Mountain has become an anchor for Cramer Mountain Country Club and the mountainside is dotted with luxury homes. Despite the influx of people, the town of Cramerton maintains its historic and unique flavor, a refreshing friendliness.

Belmont has established a train museum complete with restored cars. The Daniel Stowe Botanical Gardens are bursting with color and activity as the gardens are laid out and the tours are established.

New and diversified business has put down roots in Gaston County. Freightliner rolled its truck manufacturing plants into the county more than 10 years ago. Computer software firms have set up shop. A furniture manufacturer has moved near Stanley. Cities and towns have set aside acres and acres of land for industrial parks and industrial development, and industry is taking advantage of the welcome mat to move in and set up.

All has not been milk and honey; however, and Gaston County residents have had some frightening moments as weather-related incidents seemed destined to wreck everything they had built. Once again the pioneer spirit of conquering adversity was challenged, and the people rose to the call.

Early in the morning before first light on September 22, 1989, a hurricane blew into Gaston County twisting tree trunks out of the ground, turning trailer parks into heaps of almost unrecognizable metal, snatching the roofs off some houses and reducing others to hopeless piles of sticks. For days Gaston County was crippled. Many of its citizens were without electricity and water as they began the cleanup from Hurricane Hugo. Trees lay across the roadways, power lines crackled and sputtered until they died but remained hazardous for motorists who feared crossing them. Nearly every house sported some sort of colorful tarpaulin somewhere on its roof or across its windows, and carpenters became the most sought-after people in the county.

Again Gaston County rose to the challenge of picking up and starting over. Neighbor helped neighbor. The sound of chainsaws roared through the county from sunup to sundown and sometimes into the night beyond. The sharing and caring that has marked this county from its earliest days continued, and once again the county bandaged and healed its sores and survived.

The scars left by Hurricane Hugo on Gaston's piece of the earth are, for the most part, gone. New construction has claimed part of the devastated woods; new growth of trees and underbrush the rest. But the memory of that early morning blast will remain in the minds and hearts of the residents forever. So will the caring they showed for each other. Stories of loss and of survival will follow to the next generations.

Despite setbacks, the progress continues, marking the 1990s with change and challenge.

Always the industrious ones, long-time residents of Gaston County, some whose heritage dates 200 years, have established businesses and industries. Some are support industries for the larger ones that have moved in. Others are retail outfits that supply the needs of those who live in Gaston County.

New highways circle cities, towns, and communities, speeding up the

❑ *The Belmont Train Museum is an interesting attraction, complete with restored cars. Photo by Jim Brown, Jr. #718*

❑ *The Daniel Stowe Botanical Gardens are a beautiful tribute to one of the area's founding entrepreneurs. Courtesy of Mike Bush and Stowe Botanical Gardens. #735*

movement of goods to another area or into Gaston. Train tracks still criss-cross the county, but so do truck routes, other ground support systems, and air freight routes—all things that have helped to make the business pulse of Gaston County beat as strongly as the heart of a patriot as he carved his heritage out of the raw land.

Education, public and private, is on the cutting edge of new technology, offering the student the best of everything in his or her quest for knowledge and a secure place in the coming century. Neighborhoods, new and old, are flourishing. New houses go up every day, and old ones get fresh coats of paint and tender loving care.

The industry, the leadership, the citizenship, and the heartbeat of Gaston County are strong, ready for the challenges and rewards the 21st century is sure to bring.❑

❑ *Industry, retail, and new housing developments all demonstrate that Gaston County is still growing. Photo by Jim Brown, Jr. #725*

Partners In Progress

Sisters Of Mercy Of the Americas

*The **Sisters of Mercy** have been in Gaston County for more than 100 years.*

The Sisters of Mercy have been in Gaston County for more than 100 years, overseeing a diverse group of ministries in education, health care, and social work. The Motherhouse in Belmont is headquarters for the Regional Community of North Carolina. This includes 140 sisters and 52 associates throughout North Carolina and Guam, where foundation was made in 1946.

Their history is actually two histories, one that began in Ireland in 1831 and another that began in Charleston, South Carolina, in 1829. The Sisters of Mercy of the Americas—North Carolina originated from the Sisters of Charity of Our Lady of Mercy, founded by Bishop John England in Charleston. Three sisters from that community came to North Carolina first during the Civil War to nurse victims of yellow fever in Wilmington, and later to start a school there. The sisters founded a school in Hickory and then moved from Wilmington to Belmont where they would be closer to the services of the Church. In 1892, the sisters opened a convent and an academy in Belmont.

In 1913, they became affiliated with the Sisters of Mercy founded by Catherine McAuley in Dublin, Ireland, because they shared a similar ministry. Catherine was a wealthy young woman who dedicated her life to helping the many poor women and children who came to the city of Dublin in the 1800s.

The Belmont school, first chartered in 1904 as Sacred Heart Academy and in 1909 as Sacred Heart College, grew into a junior college in 1935 and into a senior college in 1965. The academy, the college, and the elementary school have now ceased academic operation. The sisters' resources have been shifted to their other programs, and new ones have begun. Sisters of Mercy sponsored institutions on the Belmont campus today are:

• Holy Angels, Inc., which got its start when a young mother brought her handicapped child to the sisters' day-care center in the 1950s. The Sisters persuaded physicians and others to help establish a permanent home for other handicapped children. In addition to this residential center which provides health care, treatment, and developmental training for mentally retarded and multiply handicapped children from infancy through 18 years old, there are now six group homes; The Maria Morrow Center, a treatment and education program; and Little Angels Child Development Center.

• House of Mercy, Inc., which includes a six-bed residence providing care for homeless persons living with AIDS and a case management program for non-residents in Gaston and surrounding counties;

• The McAuley Center which offers adult religious education and retreats to address the spiritual needs of the people in the Diocese of Charlotte;

• Mercy Institute/Well of Mercy, which provides individual and group therapy and psycho-spiritual growth programs for adults; and

• Catherine's House, a transitional housing facility that offers housing and support programs for women and/or women with children who are homeless.

In addition to these programs and institutions in Belmont, the Sisters of Mercy staff elementary schools and a high school elsewhere in the state, sponsor three general hospitals in North Carolina, and minister in parishes, diocesan offices, colleges, and other institutions in this state and others. On Guam, Rota, and Saipan, sisters minister in schools, nurseries, a hospital, a university, the public school system, a senior citizens center, parishes, and dioceses.❑

*The **Sisters of Mercy** opened a convent & an academy in Belmont in 1892.*

Gaston County

Gaston County, one of the most important areas in the country's textile industry, has undergone several transformations since it was created by the North Carolina State legislature in 1846. Sixth in population among the state's one hundred counties, Gaston has more than 175,000 residents. The county has fifteen incorporated towns, the most of any county in North Carolina.

The county was named for William Gaston who served in the State Senate, State House, and U.S. House of Representatives. Gaston also served as North Carolina Supreme Court judge from 1833-1844. He wrote the state song, "The Old North State."

Catawba Indians lived in the area before it was settled in the mid-1700s by pioneers of Scotch Irish, Pennsylvania Dutch, and English descent. Anticipating an attack by the Cherokees who were engaged in border warfare, early settlers constructed a fort at the junction of the Catawba and South Fork Rivers. However, relations with the few Native Americans in the area remained friendly. There is no evidence the fort was ever necessary.

Small, self-sufficient farms were developed in Gaston County, but the area never experienced the agricultural prosperity known in other parts of the state due to low crop yields. Corn, one of the most abundant crops, was converted into whiskey by 48 licensed distilleries in the county. By 1870 Gaston was known as the "Banner Corn Whiskey County of Carolina." In addition to the distilleries, mines in various parts of the county yielded gold, lime, sulphur, tin, and iron. Furnaces for smelting ore were located near what became the cities of Mount Holly, Bessemer City, and High Shoals.

The county's industrial boom had its origins in the 1840s and 1850s, when the first three cotton mills were established. The first mill was established by Thomas Tate who placed spinning machinery in his mill at Mountain Island on the Catawba River. This area is the present site of Duke Power Company's Mountain Island steam plant. The other two mills were located on the South Fork River. Near present day McAdenville the Lineberger family and others established Woodlawn Factory, known locally as the "Pinhook Mill." The Stowe Factory was situated a few miles down river.

Industrialization grew after the turn of the century, and Gaston County became known as the "combed yarn capital of the country." It still leads all other counties in the nation in the number of spindles in operation and the number of bales of cotton consumed.

While textiles are still the dominant industry, other manufacturers produce electrical goods, motor oil filters, chemicals, plastics, chain saws, brick and tile, zipper fasteners, business forms, resistors, corrugated boxes, lawn mowers, lithium compounds, and many other items.

Despite its heavy industrialization, Gaston County has many open, agricultural areas. A popular attraction is Crowders Mountain State Park, which includes almost 2,000 acres of woods and ridges.

The Gaston County public school system is the fifth largest in the state with an enrollment of more than 32,000 students. Institutions of higher learning include Gaston College, a county-supported community college; Belmont Abbey College, a Catholic liberal arts institution; and the North Carolina Center for Applied Textile Technology.

To enhance the educational and cultural life of its citizens, the county supports the Museum of Art and History in Dallas, the Public Library system, and the Recreation and Parks Department.❏

(L to R) Charles Moore, County Attorney; David Ward Jr., Commissioner; Jerry Crisp, Commissioner; Geraldine Conner, Commissioner; Porter L. McAteer, Commissioner; Gene A. Miller, Commissioner; Patricia Ellis, Commissioner; Caroleen Kuykendoll, Commissioner; Philip L. Hinely, County Manager.

City of Gastonia

A classic "new South" city, the City of Gastonia was incorporated in 1877, the year reconstruction ended. The empetus for the early development of Gastonia was the combined effect of the arrival of the railroad and the introduction of the steam powered textile mill. Today, Gastonia is the second largest city in the Charlotte metropolitan area (Charlotte-Gastonia-Rock Hill SMA) and is still considered the fine combed yarn capital of the world.

Throughout its history, Gastonia has been associated with the textile industry, which is still the largest manufacturing sector in Gaston County. The city's reputation has been as an industrial, working-class town, but its real character is far more complex. In 1953, long before many other southern cities, minority leaders filled elected positions in Gastonia.

Over the years, the city has produced a number of statewide leaders: Governor of North Carolina, Gregg Cherry, from 1945 to 1949; and Speaker of the North Carolina House of Representatives, Carl Stewart. Former City Councilman Marshall A. Rauch served 24 years in the State Senate. Finally, Helen Marvin, the first woman from Gaston County to be elected to the State Legislature, served with distinction from 1976 to 1992. She is currently a member of the North Carolina University System Board of Governors.

Gastonia is still heavily tied to the textile industry, but the city's economic base has broadened to include other manufacturing and service industries. New industries have included international firms such as Freightliner, a division of Diamler-Benz; Wix, Inc., a division of Dana Corporation, manufacturer of automotive filters; Stabilus, Inc., gas springs manufacturer; and

Mutual of Omaha, which moved its Atlantic Regional Claims Processing Center to Gastonia from Maryland in 1991.

Retail commercial development has also become a major factor in Gastonia's continued development.

Throughout its history, Gastonia has been associated with the textile industry.

Over the past several years, Gastonia has become the major retail center for the western Charlotte metro area with over 3 million square feet of retail space in its East-end retail area, including two new 300,000-plus-square-foot shopping centers opening in the past two years and a third under construction and annexed to the city in the past two months. This new status as a retail center is reflected in a jump of almost 7 percent in retail sales in the past year.

Selected an "All American City" by the National Civic League, Gastonia offers many amenities not often found in a city of 55,000 people. Perhaps its most famous attraction is the Schiele Museum of Natural History and Planetarium. This 52,000-square-foot,

state of the art facility includes a number of large exhibit areas, a 360 degree theater, and education center. Visitors can stroll through the Catawba Village behind the museum and see how the Catawba Indians lived, visit the back-country farm for demonstrations on how 18th century settlers carved out a home in the North Carolina wilderness, and just stroll through some five areas of nature trails.

Gastonia has the advantage of having its own unique identity and history yet, with a location only 20 minutes from downtown Charlotte, it has successfully taken full advantage of industries serving the growing Charlotte metropolitan area.❑

Schiele Museum of Natural History and Planetarium.

City of Belmont

Belmont City Hall

Although Belmont was not recognized as an incorporated town until 1895, the land it occupies, called South Point, has a rich history.

South Point, the peninsula that is formed by the junction of the South Fork and Catawba rivers, was inhabited by thousands of Catawba Indians before it was settled by Europeans of Scotch-Irish and German descent. During the Revolutionary War, Major William Chronicle, who came from the Belmont area, was killed at the battle of Kings Mountain.

Many residents from the area served in the Civil War. It is believed that Nancy Hanks, mother of Abraham Lincoln, lived with her uncle near Belmont before marrying Thomas Lincoln and moving to Kentucky.

What eventually became Belmont was transformed from a strictly agricultural area to a trading center when the Southern Railway laid tracks through the area in the early 1870s. A second important development came in 1878. Leaders of the Order of St. Benedict founded a monastery known as Belmont Abbey, the beginning of today's Belmont Abbey College. The town at that time was named Garibaldi, for an Italian contractor who supplied wood and water for the railway. The name was changed to Belmont in 1895, when the city was incorporated.

In 1900, the population was 145. This was about the time the first cotton manufacturing mill was built. Belmont grew steadily over the years, with the 1990 census showing a population of 9,625. For many years, life centered around the cotton mills that employed thousands of area residents. Recently, the town has attracted new industries and residents who commute to jobs in Charlotte and Gastonia. Pa-Ted Spring Co., which manufactures springs for consumer products, moved its plant from Charlotte to Belmont. Cox Recorders, which makes electronic temperature recording devices for refrigerated tractor-trailer trucks, relocated to Belmont from Long Beach, California.

New subdivisions are being built on the south side of town. Belmont has undergone an extensive planning process to handle the new growth and preserve its distinct old neighborhoods. Well-known Miami architect and planner Elizabeth Plater-Zyberk brought a team to town to revamp Belmont's zoning ordinance, which will protect the city's historic mill villages, strengthen landscaping and screening requirements for major roads, and encourage a pedestrian-friendly environment.

Belmont has several notable landmarks. The church at Belmont Abbey is the only abbey cathedral in the United States. The stained glass windows were done by Myers Brothers Studios in Munich. They were awarded a gold prize at the World's Fair in Chicago in 1892. Another landmark on the campus is a stone slave block that was used for slave sales in pre-Civil War days.

The Sisters of Mercy Motherhouse is a large stone building on the former Sacred Heart campus. It houses 65 members of the order that directs Mercy Hospital in Charlotte, St. Joseph's Hospital in Asheville, Holy Angels Nursery in Belmont, and a number of parochial schools throughout the state. Sacred Heart was a women's college that closed in the 1980s.

Numerous civic clubs and 47 churches are located in Belmont. The city has a city manager/mayor/council form of government.❑

*The **Abbey Church of Mary** is the only abbey cathedral in the United States.*

Matthews-Belk Company

*The original **Matthews-Belk** building in downtown Gastonia.*

***Matthews-Belk** store after remodeling.*

Gastonia's Matthews-Belk Company opened in 1901 and became the largest department store in Gaston County. Matthews-Belk is part of the Belk and Leggett corporations, the largest group of family owned and operated department stores in the United States.

The flagship store is the 204,000 square-foot facility at Eastridge Mall in Gastonia, which recently underwent a multi-million dollar renovation. Its budget store, Belk Outlet Center, was moved to a spacious facility in Franklin Square shopping center in 1992. The Matthews-Belk store on the west side of town, in Dixie Village Shopping Center, was also extensively remodeled in 1992.

Two families played an important role in the history of the Matthews-Belk Company . . . the Belks and the Matthews. William Henry Belk started the first Belk Department Store in Monroe in 1888. Several years later his brother, Dr. John Belk a Union County physician, joined him in the business.

The second generation of the Belk family is still very active. John M. Belk serves as Chairman of the Board and Thomas M. Belk is President. Under their leadership, the number of Belk and Leggett stores has grown to over 300 and is the dominant department store retailer in the southeast.

The Belk Brothers expanded to Gastonia in 1901 with a store on West Main Street called Kindley/Belk Brothers, a partnership between the Belks and Will Kindley. After several years, the Belks bought out Kindley. J. Houston Matthews, Sr. joined the partnership in 1910.

The six Matthews brothers grew up in Providence Township near Charlotte. Two of them, Frank and William "Mack" Matthews joined the Belk Brothers organization in Charlotte. Two younger brothers, Oliver Matthews and Henry B. Matthews, worked at the Gastonia store. Then, under their brother J. Houston's leadership, they opened Belk stores in Montgomery, Alabama and Macon, Georgia. Only one brother, Vann Matthews, chose a different profession, becoming a physician.

J. Houston Matthews, Sr. oversaw the growth of the three-story store in Gastonia to 55,616 square feet and 275 employees by 1950. Under his leadership, Matthews-Belk Company opened a string of stores in Lincolnton, Belmont, Kings Mountain, Cherryville, and Gaffney, South Carolina; Macon, Georgia; Montgomery, Alabama; and Paris, Texas. Since that time additional stores have been opened in South Carolina, Georgia and Texas.

J. Houston Matthews, Sr. died in 1950. By that time, several of his children were active in the business. Eugene Robinson Matthews helped lead the growth of Matthews-Belk in the early 1940s. His sister, Elizabeth (now Elizabeth Matthews Welton), also had a very important leadership role in the success of Matthews-Belk. James Houston Matthews, Jr. was partner until his death in 1971, when he was succeeded by B. Frank Matthews II, who was already a leader in the organization.

The next generation continues the family's leadership. David Belk Cannon, Dr. John Belk's grandson, is a director and manager of the Gaffney, South Carolina store. B. Frank Matthews II's son, Gene R. Matthews II, is senior vice president of merchandising and store operations. Vann M. Matthews II, son of J. Houston Matthews, Jr., heads up buying for menswear.

The store stayed in downtown Gastonia until 1976, when it moved to Eastridge Mall. In 1988, Matthews-Belk Company won the Belk Organization's award for putting on the best celebration of Belk's 100th Anniversary. During the celebration, Matthews-Belk hosted a Willie Nelson concert, raised $30,000 for the United Way by hosting a special appearance benefit of Oprah Winfrey and featured all of its employees on Good Morning America.

It was a fitting celebration for Matthews-Belk Company, whose flagship store at Eastridge is the third largest store in the Belk and Leggett organization.❏

R.L. Stowe Mills, Inc.

Mr. Robert Lee Stowe

*A*t the turn of the century, Robert Lee Stowe began an enterprise that would transform Belmont into a bustling textile community. He founded Belmont's first cotton mill, starting an operation that today does sales of $80 million a year and employs 1,000 people.

The son of a Civil War veteran, Stowe began his career as a school teacher and went on to found a general mercantile store in 1889. Ten years later, he made his first investment in the fledgling cotton mill industry in Gaston County. He paid $5,000 for 50 shares of stock in the Ozark Mill in Gastonia.

Encouraged by Ozark's performance, Stowe raised $100,000 from investors to build his own operation. It was called The Chronicle Mills, named for Revolutionary War soldier Major William Chronicle, who was killed at the battle of Kings Mountain in 1780.

"He was ambitious and cognizant of the fact that agriculture would not bring this part of the country out of poverty after the Civil War," says his grandson Robert Lee Stowe III, chairman and CEO of the company.

Three months after it began production, the Chronicle plant was damaged by a cyclone. But it was successful from the start, and even in its earliest years, it paid dividends to its stockholders.

A second company, Imperial Mills, was incorporated in 1905 and became the first textile mill in North Carolina to use electricity. At about that time, Stowe's brother S.P. Stowe became vice president of the Chronicle and Imperial operations. Within two decades, the Stowes operated seven mills and owned an interest in others.

There were lean times during the depression, when R.L. Stowe Mills had 2 million pounds of yarn in its warehouses and ran just two days a week. But even then, Stowe was making shrewd business decisions. He received a loan from the federal Reconstruction Finance Corp. for $135,000 and bought the abandoned McAden Mills plant in McAdenville. It later became Pharr Yarns, operated by his son-in-law William J. Pharr, and his son Dan Stowe.

His oldest son, R.L. Stowe, Jr., joined the company in 1928, after graduating from Davidson College, and eventually became CEO. After R.L. Stowe, Jr.'s death in 1984, he was succeeded by his sons, Robert L. Stowe III, who is CEO, and Harding Stowe, who is president and chief operating officer.

The elder R.L. Stowe remained active in the company until 1959, when injuries from a fall confined him to a wheelchair. By that time, he was 93. He died just short of his 97th birthday. Stowe's influence went beyond the textile industry. He lobbied the county for better roads in the early part of the century, was an early and constant supporter of Belmont Presbyterian Church, and was named the first president of the Bank of Belmont, serving 57 years in that post. He also served 41 years as a Gaston County commissioner, 33 of those as chairman.

Like other textile operations that survived the 1970s and 1980s, R.L. Stowe Mills has invested heavily in automated equipment and continues to upgrade its facilities. In 1988, the company opened the Raymond Helms plant (named for a longtime worker), a $24 million facility that produces high-quality, ring-spun yarn comparable to the best yarns from overseas.❑

*Opened in 1988, the Raymond Helms Plant is named for a longtime employee of **R. L. Stowe Mills**.*

$\mathcal{G}$aston Federal Savings & Loan Association

Robert W. Williams,
President of Gaston Federal Savings & Loan Association, Gastonia, NC

B. Frank Matthews, II,
Chairman of the Board of Directors, Gaston Federal Savings & Loan Association, Gastonia, NC

The beginning of banking in Gastonia dates to 1887 with a private banking house named Craig and Jenkins Banking Company. Only a few of the early financial institutions have survived. Gaston Federal Savings and Loan Association is now the only federally insured mutual financial institution locally owned and operated in Gastonia, and the oldest financial institution now chartered in Gaston County. It has $150 million in assets and has helped thousands of residents realize the American dream of home ownership.

In 1904, Colonel Charles B. Armstrong, sheriff of Gaston County and a leader in textiles, organized Gastonia Mutual Building and Loan Association, the original name of Gaston Federal Savings and Loan. The first meeting of the Association was held at the Gastonia City Hall on January 5, 1905.

Gaston Federal, as a mutual institution, has no stockholders and is owned by its customers, both savers and borrowers, who are called "members." They elect the board of directors.

During its 90-year history, the Association has had only five presi-

dents or chairmen and five managing officers.

Samuel Newman Boyce served as president from 1905 until 1915. The Association's first mortgage loan was made on February 2, 1905, to J.A. Blackwood for $350. By the first annual meeting on January 4, 1906, assets were $19,333.15.

Originally headquartered in the Armstrong Company's mill office, the Association relocated to the offices of Gaston Loan and Trust Company in 1907. By 1910, assets exceeded $100,000.

The Association's second president was Samuel Alexander Robinson, who served from 1915 until his death in 1945. During his tenure, Georgia Emma Connelly was elected as the first female member of the board (1917-1919). Assets reached $500,000 by 1922.

James Guy Jackson, Sr. was elected secretary and treasurer in 1933, beginning more than four decades of his family's involvement with the institution. He retired in 1967, and his son, James G. Jackson, Jr., served as managing officer from 1968 to 1975.

The next president was Samuel McAuley Stewart, who served from 1945 to 1975. The name of the institution was changed to Gastonia Mutual Savings and Loan Association in 1959, when it had $10 million in assets. During Stewart's tenure, the association built its present home office at 245 West Main Avenue and moved there in 1971.

The fourth president was Hugh D. Whitener, Sr., who served from 1975 to

1983. The Association built its first branch office at 1535 Burtonwood Drive in 1976. It converted from a state to a federal charter and changed its name to Gaston Federal Savings and Loan Association in 1981, with assets of $68 million.

Mount Holly Federal Savings and Loan Association (formerly Mutual Building and Savings Association) merged into Gaston Federal in 1982. Assets of the combined associations exceeded $97 million.

The fifth and present chairman, B. Frank Matthews II, was elected in 1983.

The Association built its third office in Gastonia at 1670 Neal Hawkins Road in 1987. The Mount Holly branch relocated to 233 South Main Street in Mount Holly in 1990.

The current (1994) members of the board of directors are B. Frank Matthews II, State Senator David W. Hoyle, Martha Barnett Beal, James J. Fuller, William H. Keith, Charles D. Massey, Ben R. Rudisill II, and Robert W. Williams, Sr. Directors emeriti are Henry L. Fowler, Sr., Thomas M. Holland, and Hugh D. Whitener, Sr.

The current officers of the Association are B. Frank Matthews II, chairman of the board; David W. Hoyle, vice chairman; Robert W. Williams, Sr., president and chief executive officer; Paul L. Teem, Jr., executive vice president, secretary, and chief operations officer; and James A. Pittman, Jr., vice president, treasurer, and chief financial officer. Other officers are Cecil G. Berry, Mark A. Carswell II, Betty B. Gaddis, R. Scott Mullen, Lorice J. Tolbert, Martha B. Adams, Luellen P. Brown, Pamela B. Bingham, Kimberley H. Holland, and Linda M. Stewart.❏

Gaston Health Care

Gastonia's first hospital was located in a boarding house on Airline Avenue.

Gastonia's first hospital was established in 1908 in a boarding house on Airline Avenue. Over the years, it evolved into what is now Gaston Health Care, Inc., the parent of seven affiliated companies.

The cornerstone is Gaston Memorial Hospital, a 442-bed acute-care facility serving residents of Gaston County and surrounding areas. It employs more than 1,800 health care and support personnel and serves more than 100,000 patients each year.

All this began when three doctors opened City Hospital on Airline Avenue with nine beds. Several years later, the hospital moved to the third floor of the Realty Building on Main Street, and then in 1924, a new City Hospital was built on North Highland Street with 46 beds.

Gaston Memorial was conceived 20 years later, when returning veteran Brown Wilson came up with the idea of a living memorial to Gaston County men who had lost their lives in World War II. Adopted as a project by the American Legion Post in Gastonia, the hospital was supported by public subscription, and its name was changed in 1946 to Gaston Memorial.

It was clear by the early 1960s that Gaston County needed more modern facilities. The new hospital, opened in December 1973, was constructed at a cost of $17.1 million, including $2.1 million in state and federal funds.

Gaston Memorial is licensed for 442 beds, offering all private patient rooms. A four-level addition opened in 1992, which houses The Birthplace, a 28-suite unit that allows all maternity care in one room, as well as a Level II Emergency Department that features 28 treatment areas and a helipad for air transport.

In 1993, Gaston Memorial became one of only seven hospitals in North Carolina to earn a Community Hospital Comprehensive Cancer Center designation from the American College of Surgeons. In the spring of 1994, a second linear accelerator was added to the Radiation Oncology Center, providing advanced treatment for cancer patients.

Gaston Health Care, Inc., organized in 1984, serves as the parent company of Gaston Memorial Hospital and six affiliated companies, including:
- The Diagnostic Center provides radiological and laboratory testing for outpatients, including magnetic resonance imaging and a mammography suite certified by the American College of Radiology. The Belmont Diagnostic Center, a satellite center located in The Belmont Medical Building, provides outpatient radiologic and laboratory testing for patients with physicians in eastern Gaston County.
- Gaston Health Resources manages a number of physicians groups, including Piedmont Health Care Associates, a family practice located in The Belmont Medical Building, Aiken-Capps Internal Medicine in Gastonia, Stanley Medical Associates in Stanley, and

The Rheumatology Center of the Piedmont in Gastonia.
- Gaston Health Services provides employee assistance services for area companies through Piedmont HealthLink, located in The Belmont Medical Building.
- Gaston Ambulatory Surgery is a free-standing same-day surgery center where low risk and minor surgeries and endoscopies are performed.
- Courtland Terrace is a 96-bed long-term nursing facility that features a section for patients requiring skilled nursing care and an assisted-living wing for patients who need only moderate nursing care.
- First Health Care Centers in Gastonia and Belmont provide care for minor burns to physical examinations and routine chest X-rays.
- GMH Home Health Care provides personal health care services for patients at home.

"Gaston Health Care continues to respond to opportunities created by the changes taking place in health care nationwide," says Wayne F. Shovelin, FACHE, president and CEO. "Gaston Health Care is in a favorable position as we work toward greater collaboration in health care." ❏

Gaston Memorial is one of the few hospitals in North Carolina to earn a Community Hospital Comprehensive Cancer Center designation.

Gaston Chamber of Commerce

The year was 1913. The textile industry was just starting to pick up momentum in Gaston County. And the Chamber of Commerce, then known as the Board of Trade, held its first meeting.

One hundred and ninety businessmen paid an initiation fee of $10 to be charter members, with T.C. Craig serving as the first president and O.A. Lloyd, the first secretary. The group rented office space at Gaston Loan and Trust Co.

Since that first meeting, the Gaston Chamber of Commerce has compiled a long record of working to attract industry and recognizing local businesses for their achievements. It has lobbied to improve roads and utilities services, and has been a strong supporter of education.

In recent years, the Chamber has expanded its role in the community. Tim Helms took over as president in 1991 and began an aggressive campaign to increase membership and establish new programs. Since then, membership has grown from 600 to 1,000 members.

The Chamber sponsors a wide range of activities, including a monthly Business After Hours program, a First Friday Breakfast, and a Wednesday luncheon lecture. The Chamber held its first Business Expo in 1992, which allowed local firms to demonstrate their products and services to Chamber members and other businesses. There were 150 booths at the 1993 expo.

The Chamber also hosts a Christmas show to promote local business. It plans environmental seminars so companies can share ideas on how they're reducing waste and pollution.

Another important part of the Chamber's mission is promoting education. Under a program set up by the Gaston Chamber, all 54 schools in the county have been adopted by one or more businesses that provide the schools with money, speakers, and support for teachers. A mentor program identifies at-risk children and matches them with adults. Helms oversees all Chamber programs, along with Viviana Brunnemer, vice president for membership and marketing. The chairman of the Chamber board for 1994 is Dr. Loretta Dodgen, managing partner of Multiple Choice.

Before Helms took over, Phil Coyle directed Chamber activities for 15 years. A number of new industrial areas were established during that time. The Chamber helped work out a grant system with the county that allowed utility expansion near Mount Holly, Stanley, Dallas, and Bessemer City.

The Look Up Gaston Campaign, begun in the late 1970s, was

Gaston Chamber of Commerce circa 1957.

who headed up Look Up Gaston for several years.

In the 1980s, the Chamber led a campaign to legalize the sale of alcoholic beverages at restaurants. Since then, dozens of new restaurants have opened in Gastonia.

The Chamber built its present office on West Franklin Boulevard in 1954 after occupying an office on Main Street in downtown Gastonia. The office underwent extensive renovations in 1991-1992.❏

Early Chamber leaders.

*The **Gaston Chamber of Commerce** staff focuses on building a strong industrial community and recognizing local businesses for their achievements.*

important in improving the county's image and identifying important issues. Its programs included a leadership development program and the beautification of city streets with crepe myrtle and Bradford pear trees. It was also an important forum, bringing all the mayors in Gaston County together for the first time and conducting numerous citizen surveys.

"It began to give citizens the feeling they were helping determine what was going on," says Phil Coyle, a former executive with the Chamber

Parkdale Mills

*An award presented to **Parkdale Mills** by the City of Gastonia for appearance of grounds and building.*

The history of Parkdale Mills can be told through workers like Eula Brazell, who spent 42 years at the company.

She was born in one of the company owned houses and joined Parkdale at age 16, near the end of World War II. The two-story, red-brick plant was making yarn that went into uniforms for the armed services.

In 1951, Parkdale was the first cotton mill to be air-conditioned, a change that gave Brazell a relief from stifling hot summer days. In 1961, Duke Kimbrell, who had started doing odd jobs at the mill when he was 15, became president of Parkdale. The next three decades saw dramatic expansion that made Parkdale the biggest producer of yarns in the United States with some of the most modern technology.

Brazell and her husband, who worked for Parkdale 48 years, always felt they had secure jobs. "It made a living for us," says Brazell. "We bought our home, we have two cars, we sent our daughter to college."

These days, the company makes a living for 2,200 employees in 21 cotton and cotton-blend yarn-manufacturing plants. Parkdale produces more than 300 million pounds of yarn a year. "Parkdale has always been noted as the first textile plant to put in the latest

equipment," says Eula Brazell.

Parkdale was organized about 11 years before Kimbrell was born, by two prominent textile families in Gastonia, the Greys and the Separks. The original mill was completed in 1918 and employed 200 people making 40,000 pounds of cotton thread per week.

When the founders had financial difficulties, Lee Robinson of National Bank of Commerce foreclosed on the families' mills and distributed the stock to his sons. William Robinson ended up with the majority share of Parkdale's stock and took over as chief executive in the 1930s.

Parkdale continued to produce yarn for threads until 1940, when the government required the mill to switch to yarn for gabardine fabric, which was produced at Cramerton Mills and eventually went into soldiers' uniforms.

This was an important turning point, because it allowed Parkdale to mass produce a certain kind of yarn rather than have to make different kinds of thread yarn for different customers. The plant remained on Second Avenue, now Garrison Boulevard. By 1941, Parkdale produced about 85,000 pounds of yarn a week.

Kimbrell went to work for Parkdale

during school vacations at age 15. After graduating from Gastonia High School, he joined the Air Force and served as a gunner in the 493rd Bomb Squadron stationed in Ipswich, England. After Kimbrell was discharged, William Robinson and Chuck Adams advised him to major in textiles at North Carolina State University, where he earned a degree in three years.

Several managers were key to the company's growth at that time. Chuck Adams was vice president of manufacturing. Dave Dellinger, A.J. Redman, and C.L. Cline all worked as supervisors under Adams. "They were the backbone of making the company come through in good standing," says Kimbrell.

The original building was expanded, and in 1951 Parkdale air-conditioned its plant, a change that made equipment run more smoothly and vastly improved morale. "When you're working in a more desirable environment, it changes your outlook," says Brazell.

Production was up to 140,000 pounds of yarn a week in 1955. Parkdale focused on mass producing a few counts (diameters) of yarn. This improved efficiency and by 1960 production was up to 200,000 pounds a week, and the plant was further expanded. Duke Kimbrell had gradually moved up in the company. When Robinson died in 1961, Kimbrell, who had already been running the company, took over as chief executive officer.

Unable to expand the original mill any more, Parkdale built its second mill adjacent to the first in 1964. By the mid-1960s, Parkdale employed 700 people and produced 300,000 pounds of yarn a week. The second mill was doubled in size in 1967, upping production to 400,000 pounds a week.

A big change was occurring in the apparel industry—the introduction of permanent-press fabrics made from a blend of cotton and polyester. Kimbrell convinced his board of directors to purchase Erlanger Mills in Lexington, a corduroy operation about to go into bankruptcy. Parkdale discarded Erlanger's weaving equipment and replaced it with machinery to make cotton and polyester-blend yarn for the knitting trade.

A lot was at stake. It was Parkdale's first venture outside of Gastonia and its first expansion into a product other than 100 percent cotton yarn.

"If we had failed, they would have fired me," says Kimbrell.

But Erlanger was profitable within a year, and it's now the biggest, most profitable mill that Parkdale owns, producing 1,300,000 pounds a week. It set the stage for further expansion. Over the next two decades, Kimbrell

Parkdale Mills' Textile Week display at Eastridge Mall Gastonia, NC.

*Retiree's meet regularly to share a meal and talk about their memories of working at **Parkdale**.*

oversaw the acquisition of 17 more plants within an hour's drive on Interstate 85.

The next purchase was Mauney Mills in Kings Mountain, another company in financial difficulty. It was renovated and began producing cotton-polyester yarns. Then came two plants in Thomasville in 1976. The stockholders of the owner, Amazon Mills, were in bankruptcy when Parkdale bought the operation.

Kimbrell and Bill Robinson's daughter, Douglas Robinson Henry, gained control of the company in a leveraged buy out in 1982. Kimbrell continued to look for acquisitions.

In the 1980s, Parkdale purchased five mills from the Harold Lineberger family, including one in Salisbury and four in Belmont. Parkdale also bought a plant from MFB Knitting Co., the old RCG Love mill, on East Ozark Street and converted it from knitting to yarn production.

The MFB plant allowed Parkdale to increase its production of open-end yarns, a process that produces a somewhat coarser, less expensive yarn more quickly than ring-spun yarn. The market for open-end yarn had been growing ever since Parkdale began using the process in the 1970s. It costs at least 20 percent less than ring-spun yarn and works well in certain fabrics.

There were more purchases. In 1989, the Pinckney Stowe family sold its three Belmont Heritage mills to Parkdale, which converted them from ring-spun to open-end spinning. In 1991, Parkdale bought two mills from Martinsville, Virgina-based Tultex in Lowell and Kings

Parkdale Associates in Washington, DC, for Textile rally.

Mountain. In the next two years, Parkdale also bought a plant from Delta Woodside between Gastonia and Bessemer City and two plants from Bassett Walker in Monroe and Mineral Springs. In 1990, the company built a Fiber Distribution Center in Belmont that allows it to receive all its cotton at one location and do a better job of blending it before it goes to yarn production.

Parkdale continues to invest in technology at all of its plants. The new technology requires more highly skilled workers. Parkdale will no longer hire high school dropouts under the age of 19 unless they agree to finish their high school equivalency.

Kimbrell's son-in-law, Anderson Warlick, is president and chief operating officer. The company is active in a wide range of nonprofit organizations and was a top supporter of United Way in 1993.

By reinvesting profits, acquiring new technology, training good leaders, and sticking to a simple product line, Parkdale has survived and prospered in a time when foreign competition has forced many others out of business.❑

$\mathcal{S}$andoz Chemicals Corporation

$\mathcal{F}$or almost 60 years, North Carolinians have been making some of the world's finest dyes and chemicals right here on the banks of the Catawba River—just across from Mount Holly, North Carolina—where many Sandoz employees live, raise families, do their shopping, and go to church.

It was across the river from Mount Holly that John L. Crist founded Southern Dyestuffs Company—later called Sodyeco—to develop and manufacture liquid sulfur dyes in the heart of the U.S. textile industry.

Crist, a native of Virginia, and 1912 graduate of Washington and Lee University, came to the Mount Holly area with over 20 years of textile industry experience. His invention of liquid sulfur dye was a vast improvement over the powder form that was commonly used. The powder dye was mixed with water and sodium sulfide and heated, a process that was messy and time consuming.

"He was ahead of his time," says retired company attorney, Wilton Rankin. "He believed the only reason you were in business was to serve customers. You could call Crist, and he'd have the dye to you within an hour."

The business Crist founded in 1936 is now part of Sandoz Chemicals Corporation, a major U.S. producer of specialty chemicals and dyes, particularly sulfur-based dyes for the textile industry.

Sulfur dyes are widely used on cotton fabrics such as denim blue jeans. In fact, about nine out of every 10 pairs of blue jeans are dyed with sulfur dyes. Dyes for other consumer products such as leather goods and footwear are also made at the Mount Holly plant.

Sandoz is a major U.S. producer of specialty chemicals and dyes used by the textile industry.

Today, the Mount Holly plant is the largest of six Sandoz Chemicals facilities making dyes and chemicals in the United States. The plant occupies seven buildings on the original site and employs over 350 people. Sandoz' commitment to safety of its employees, environmental protection, and quality is evident in many ways. For example, the site has received numerous safety and quality awards from government agencies and customers. And, the environmental team at the plant has converted two of the plant's old wastewater treatment lagoons into an award-winning wildlife habitat.

In addition, the Mount Holly plant was recently registered to the standards of ISO 9001, meaning that the quality systems of the plant meet rigorous international quality standards.

Sandoz Mount Holly plant employees have a long tradition of involvement in community life, through volunteer work in such vital areas as tutoring in local schools, charitable contributions, and by active participation in local fire-fighting efforts. The company supports these efforts and makes contributions to similar groups.

By making investments of this type in the community, Sandoz Chemicals commits its long-term support to the Gaston community.◻

Sandoz Chemicals Corporation is located on the banks of the Catawba River.

McLean & Son Funeral Home

When the late Will G. McLean finished Brown College of Embalming in Raleigh, in 1925, he became Gaston County's first licensed embalmer. As a young man, he established McLean & Son Funeral Home, now operated by the family's third and fourth generations.

"He was very particular in how our families were served. As a young boy, he instilled in me those principles of service," says William J. "Bill" McLean, Jr., grandson of the founder.

The elder McLean took his grip and portable cooling board (embalming table) to the homes of families throughout the county. Chemicals are now purchased commercially, but in those days embalmers formulated their own. Funeral homes were a new development in the 1920s, and McLean was a pioneer in the business.

He took on several partners in the 1920s and 1930s, including Ervin Carothers, Talmadge Settlemyer, and John Rhyne. McLean Undertaking Co. was located in a building on Franklin Avenue in downtown Gastonia, in what is now O.G. Penegar Co.

During that period, Gaston County imported hundreds of employees from the North Carolina mountains to work in the growing textile industry. Families still had ties to their old homes, and they frequently asked that the deceased be transported by hearse back to the mountains.

McLean Undertaking Co. moved to 206 S. Broad Street in 1947. McLean's son, William J. McLean, Sr., became a partner in 1938, and the name of the business was changed to McLean & Son Funeral Home. In the late 1950s, a funeral chapel was added to the building.

Third generation William J. "Bill" McLean, Jr. was already active in the business as a teenager, helping move equipment and do other jobs. He remembers going with his father when embalming was still done occasionally in homes. He joined the business officially in 1962, after graduating from the Cincinnati College of Embalming.

The family has a long tradition in serving as coroner to the county. The founder was coroner from 1940 until his death in 1953, when his son was appointed to fill his term. In 1966, William McLean, Jr. was elected to replace his father.

The company expanded in 1978, when it affiliated with Bumgardner Funeral Home, which was once part of the D.P. Stowe Co., and has provided funeral service to Belmont since 1870. In 1988, fourth generation William J. McLean III was named manager and vice president of the Belmont operation, now known as McLean-Bumgardner Funeral Home.

McLean & Son has long been active in state and national trade associations. In 1970, the company was invited to join the National Selected Morticians, a group of independently owned and operated funeral-service firms that audits and inspects member firms annually.

William J. "Bill" McLean's wife, Eva Ann Orr McLean, a licensed funeral director, is secretary/vice president of the firm.❑

McLean & Son Broad Street facility circa 1947 was the former home of John O. Rankin.

Choice USA Beverage, Inc.

As a child walking home from school in the 1940s, Jim Falls occasionally dropped by The Orange Crush Bottling Co., where owner C.P. Nanney treated him and other children to Double Colas.

Years later, Falls returned to the bottling company, this time to buy the business and build it into a modern facility. The company is now known as Choice USA Beverage, Inc.

The company's signature soft drink is Sun-drop, the popular citrus drink as closely identified with Gastonia as the textile industry. For many years, the business was known as the Sun-drop Bottling Co., and it is still the biggest bottler of Sun-drop in the country.

The company is also seen as a strong corporate citizen. Choice USA is a longtime supporter of the United Way, Salvation Army, YMCA, and many other civic organizations. This involvement began with C.P. Nanney, who got into the bottling business in the 1920s and became partners with the brothers L.L. and M.O. Mingus. Nanney bought out the Mingus brothers in 1939. He left his first building on Long Avenue and built a new plant on East Franklin, where he bottled Orange Crush, Double Cola, Nugrape, Cheerwine, and exotic flavors like peach and hot ginger.

(Left) Mr. Powell Nanney, (Right) Mr. J.P. Falls

"Mr. Nanney had a real acute palate," remembers Falls. "He would take Double Cola and pour a little on the cement floor. He could tell from the fizz when it hit the concrete floor if the carbonation was right."

C.P. Nanney's nephew, Powell Nanney, went to work for the company in 1946 and now serves as vice chairman of the board of directors. He remembers when the company became the first bottler of Sun-drop in the country in 1953. "Sales were in the area of Coke and Pepsi," recalls Powell Nanney. "In the beginning there was no advertising, just word of mouth."

The company, which had been known as various combinations of the names Orange Crush and Double Cola Bottling Co., changed to Sun-drop Bottling Co. By 1960, about 44 employees worked at the Gastonia plant.

As C.P. Nanney approached retirement age, he re-met Jim Falls, then a young stock broker, and offered to sell him the company in 1970. Within nine days of buying the facility, Falls decided to invest in all new machinery, spending twice the net worth of the company. Nanney stayed on for the next decade as his mentor. "I knew finance, but I knew absolutely nothing about bottling," says Falls. "I had 10 years of tutoring by Mr. Nanney."

In the early 1970s, the company had about 90 employees. Falls was distributing many national brands which included Sun-Drop, Cheerwine, and the Crush line of products, but he already had in mind the idea of manufacturing private-label soft drinks for other companies. When the company

*(Left) Mr. C. P. Nanney, original owner of The Orange Crush Bottling Co.; Mr.J.P. Falls, current owner of **Choice USA Beverage, Inc.***

began to run out of space in the 1980s, Falls bought the old Coca-Cola Bottling Co. building on Franklin and moved Choice USA's sales and administrative offices there. The 1990s have seen the previous ideas of the 1970s come to reality, as Falls now produces soft drinks for such well known companies as Wal-Mart, Pharmor, and Family Dollar.

The company came out with the Choice brand of products in 1987 and changed its name to Choice USA.

Choice USA, which employs over 100 people, is run by Falls, his son, Jay Falls, and Executive Vice President Sam Robinson.

It is still thought of as a family institution. "I may have bought the company," says Falls, "but in this town this is still Mr. Nanney's company."❏

Southeastern Credit Bureau, Inc.

Southeastern Credit Bureau, Inc. was one of the first merchant associations in the state of North Carolina.

Southeastern Credit Bureau, Inc. in Gastonia was established in 1924 as one of the first merchant associations in the state of North Carolina.

Southeastern Credit Bureau, Inc., provides credit reporting services to businesses in Gaston, Lincoln, and Cleveland counties and numerous counties in Tennessee. It also provides mortgage reporting and collection services throughout the northeast and southeast.

Credit reporting was a strictly local need in the early years. Shoppers rarely made purchases in more than a 20-mile radius from home, resulting in many small towns forming their own local merchants associations. Fourteen local grocers which needed help with credit reporting and collections organized the West Gastonia Merchants Association which was operated from the back of Blanton's Grocery Store.

As the business grew, the Merchants Association moved to different locations downtown, finally locating in what was once the Women's Club Building in 1970.

Then in 1982, the association was purchased by Southeastern Credit Bureau, Inc., headquartered in Kannapolis, North Carolina.

In the early years, credit reporting clients requested credit information by telephone. This required an employee to manually record the inquiry, locate the credit report from a file cabinet, then provide the client with a verbal or manually updated credit report. Computers revolutionized the credit reporting industry in the 1970s and 1980s. Today, clients access numerous credit products via computer systems in a near totally automated environment.

Southeastern Credit Bureau, Inc., became affiliated with Equifax in 1982, which gave the company access to more than 200 million credit files throughout the United States and United Kingdom. Equifax, is one of the country's three largest credit reporting agencies.

Southeastern Credit Bureau, Inc. grew rapidly in the 1980s. The company left its building at 105 W. Second in 1992 and renovated what used to be the Western District office of the Boy Scouts of America. The 12,000-square-foot brick building was built by the Works Progress Administration, one of President Franklin D.

Roosevelt's New Deal programs. In 1993, once again squeezed for space, Southeastern Credit Bureau, Inc. relocated it's credit reporting and mortgage reporting divisions back to the 105 W. Second location.

Additionally, the mortgage service division provides mortgage reports to mortgage loan centers across the southeast. This service is provided in a total electronic environment.

The collection service division, once a courtesy service to its members, is now a major thrust of the organization. Southeastern utilizes the most state of the art telecommuications, computer, and collection software systems in the country. Southeastern Credit Bureau, Inc., handles collection accounts for utilities companies, retail businesses, medical facilities, and others across the eastern seaboard.

Southeastern Credit Bureau, Inc., continues to excel in their involvement in a wide range of civic and professional organizations. For example, Southeastern Credit Bureau, Inc.'s associates have served as Past Presidents of Associated Credit Bureau, Inc. and Credit Professionals. Additionally, they currently serve on numerous industry advisory committees and local civic organizations.❏

Main operations building located at 113 W. Third Avenue.

Carothers Funeral Home

The history of Carothers Funeral Home spans almost 60 years and includes three generations of the founding family.

Ervin Carothers started the business in 1928. He worked in a textile mill in Rock Hill as a young man, but felt he was destined to be either a minister or a funeral director. He left the mill to work for McLean Undertaking Co. in Gastonia in 1925 and later organized Carothers Funeral Home on Franklin Avenue.

Today, Carothers is part of the Loewen Group, Inc. of British Columbia. The Carothers Holding Company, formed in 1990, operates 49 funeral homes and 11 cemeteries in the Carolinas, Virginia, and Georgia. Buddy Carothers, Ervin Carothers' nephew, and his wife Phyllis are part owners.

Between the time Ervin Carothers founded the funeral home and Loewen bought it, numerous changes and expansions took place. Two brothers, J.C. Carothers and E. Woodrow Carothers, joined the funeral home in the 1930s. Ervin formed a partnership with C.T. Settlemyer in 1936 and made several acquisitions—the Wilson residence on Franklin Avenue, and funeral homes in Mount Holly, Belmont, and Stanley. W. Gray McArver was the first manager of the Belmont operation. His son, Jeff McArver, also worked as a manager for the company from 1948 to 1993.

The fourth Carothers brother, Luther Carothers, joined the company after serving in World War II and became manager of the Mount Holly location until his retirement in 1987.

Buddy Carothers, son of J.C., lived on the second floor of the Wilson residence, over the funeral home, as a child. He joined the company as an apprentice in 1952 after graduating from the Cincinnati College of Mortuary Science. His cousin, Woody Carothers, Jr., began his career in 1962 after graduating from the Dallas Institute of Mortuary Science. The business moved from the Wilson home to a 14,000-square-foot brick building on Second and Chester in 1959.

Expansion continued. Carothers acquired the Dallas Funeral Home in 1974, the York Funeral Home in 1981, and the 110-year-old Grey and Daniel Cotton Co. building at Second and Chester in 1986. The Carothers and Williams family, owner of Gaston Memorial Parks, merged their firms in 1986, forming the Carothers-Williams Company.

In order to continue the growth pattern the company formed a partnership; Carothers Holding Company, Inc. with The Loewen Group, Inc. in British Columbia, Canada. The local partners are Phyllis & Buddy Carothers, with Buddy serving as Managing Partner and President. The board of directors includes Ray Loewne, Peter Hyndman and Buddy Carothers.

Bill Rinehart, who joined Carothers as an apprentice in 1958, serves as regional manager for the company. Harris High is regional controller, Phyllis Carothers is vice president, and Buddy Carothers is president and divisional vice president for the parent company. Woodie Carothers, Jr. is vice president and manager of Carothers in Gastonia. Woodie Carothers' wife, Brenda, is also a funeral director.

The third generation involved in the company is Buddy and Phyllis' daughter Beth Carothers, who graduated with an associate degree in mortuary science from The Gupton Jones College of Mortuary Science in 1993 and works as a funeral director.

Carothers Funeral Home's emphasis today is on providing spacious facilities, an up-do-date fleet, and funeral planning services. Advanced planning allows clients to set up a trust account or insurance policy that fixes the price of their funeral arrangements. Sharing sessions are offered by a trained counselor to help clients deal with their loss.❑

*The history of the **Carothers Funeral Home** spans three generations of the founding family.*

Watson Insurance

Founder Craig Watson believed that dedication & personal service has given his company the dependable reputation it enjoys today.

For residents of Gastonia, September 22, 1989 will always be remembered as the day Hurricane Hugo struck.

Hugo did more than $120 million in damage to Gaston County. Thousands of homes went without electricity or water for days. Schools closed. Businesses were forced to close until repairs could be done.

There was one office that opened at 8:30 a.m. on the Saturday after the hurricane struck and kept its regular schedule in the weeks afterwards. It was Watson Insurance, a company founded in 1934. Watson Insurance set up extra space to file claims and assure customers their losses would be covered. The years that Watson Insurance had been in business gave the company the strength and skill to handle the enormous challenge of such a disaster.

As founder Craig Watson said, "We never allowed ourselves to get too big. When I get a request from one of my insureds, I take care of it personally. It may look silly for me to go out and deliver a $10 policy, but it hurts me to see a $10 policy lost through indifference."

Watson was a young man of the depression when he purchased R.O. Crawford to start his own company. He had arrived in Gastonia from Wildwood, North Carolina, when he was 10, to be raised by an aunt and uncle. Watson's first job was as a "runner" for the Gaston Loan and Trust Company, delivering deposits to the Federal Reserve Bank in Charlotte. The bank's insurance department was sold to Crawford, who ran the division for the bank and later was purchased by Watson.

Watson was confident, driven, and focused from the day he sold his first policy. Family members tell of the time he was driving in the Firestone area, a large mill community, when he saw fire trucks at one home. He drove straight to the house, reassured the family, wrote a personal check for their policy and handed it to them with a flourish.

"That was infinitely good service," says Tom Watson, son of the founder and now chief executive.

Business grew steadily in the 1940s and 1950s, enabling the company to move from its original office over Gene's Soda Shop on Main Street to two different downtown locations, one on South Marietta and the other on East Franklin. Then, in 1967, the company moved into its current building at Second Avenue and Broad Street. The office was built to accomodate a second story which doubled the square footage in 1988.

In 1967, the agency consisted of 31 employees, including several World War II combat veterans. Cliff Broome, then vice president of the N.C. Association of Mutual Insurance Agents, was Watson's right-hand man.

Broome, who retired after 43 years, remembers Watson as "one of the best salesmen I ever saw in my life." He also remembers him as someone who stressed education, and always believed it was a good investment to pay for employees' continuing education.

The late 1970s were a time when a number of women at Watson Insurance went on to continue their education. Peggy Hutchins, who began as Craig Watson's secretary in the early 1960s, is now head of administration for the commercial insurance department and a Certified Property and Casualty Underwriter (CPCU), the highest education ranking for insurance professionals.

"It gave me a really good feeling about myself," says Hutchins, "and an excellent understanding of what is involved in writing an insurance program for a client." She is one of eight CPCUs in the company.

Watson Insurance deals with 25 major carriers, and dozens of others for special coverage. It serves 15,000 personal insurance clients and 3,000 business clients—ranging from international manufacturing companies to small family-owned businesses.

The company opened its first branch office in the early 1960s and now operates four satellite locations—in Belmont, Cherryville, Mount Holly, and Lake Wylie.

In the mid 1980s, Rob and Craig Watson, III joined the firm, establishing a third generation of Watson family management. The family has long been active in civic affairs. Both Tom Watson and his father served at different times as president of the Gaston Chamber of Commerce, and they are longtime supporters of First Presbyterian Church and the United Way.

Tom Watson takes his cue from his father, who never stopped praising the value of the company's employees. When he remembers Hurricane Hugo, he talks about how most employees had damage at their own homes but rallied to help others as Watson Insurance took claims from thousands of area residents.

"We are focused on the future," says Watson. "We are very proud of where we are today." ❏

Threads USA

Victory card room of yesteryear.

*T*hreads USA had its beginnings in 1931 when 13 Gaston County textile companies organized under the name of Textiles-Incorporated and pooled their assets, equipment, and personnel to survive the Depression.

The company that became Threads USA had operated as a small department of Arkray Mill, one of the plants involved in the merger. Convinced that it would operate more efficiently as a separate entity, company leaders chartered Threads-Incorporated as a wholly owned subsidiary of Textiles-Incorporated to manufacture industrial sewing thread.

It proved to be the right decision. Threads-Incorporated prospered during the Depression and became a leading manufacturer of industrial sewing threads. Today, it is an operating group of Dixie Yarns, which acquired Ti-Caro (formerly Textiles-Incorporated) in 1987.

The company has invested heavily in equipment to speed up processes, improve products, and control inventory. Productivity in thread winding for example is four to five times what it was in the mid-1980s. The company's old winding equipment processed 250 yards of thread a minute, compared to the 1,200 to 1,400 yards a minute now possible. Automated equipment removes and replaces each cone, a procedure previously done manually.

Threads USA produces cotton and polyester threads for a wide range of apparel and other products, such as sleeping bags, tents, luggage, shoes, upholstery, baseballs, and even teabags. The company sells over 5,000 standard products to 3,500 customers located throughout the United States, as well as Europe and Latin America.

It has three plants in Gastonia and one in Puerto Rico. The Pinkney plant produces cotton yarn for sewing thread. The Victory plant produces polyester yarn for sewing thread. At the finishing plant, the yarn is dyed, lubricated, wound on thread cones, and shipped to customers. Colors are matched by computer; if the plant doesn't already have a color in stock, the computer helps develop it.

Tough demands are made on threads. The strongest can be sewn through five plies of leather and stand up to 600 F at the sewing needle.

Heavy investment in modern equipment is just part of what keeps Threads competitive. The company is also committed to upgrading the skills of workers. Every plant has a training manager.

Their job is not only to train new associates but also to work with older associates on retraining. A program was recently begun to help 150 maintenance employees master mechanical and electronic skills.

The 1,562 employees of Threads USA are encouraged to be members of quality circles, where they meet regularly and offer ideas on how to improve processes. Their teamwork doesn't end at the workplace. Each plant adopts an area school, and employees tutor children.

The history of Threads USA and its parent company mirrors changes in the textile industry in this century.

The original company, Textiles-Incorporated, combined 23 plants from 13 companies in Gaston, Cleveland, York, Mecklenburg, and Lincoln counties. The new company confined manufacturing operations to

Threads Finishing, dye department of long ago.

Gaston County and struggled to survive the Depression. Textiles-Incorporated spent 10 years in receivership, and during that time, Gastonia Banker Albert G. Myers, Sr., the company's first president, oversaw the sale and closing of several plants.

Myers is an important figure in the history of Gaston County textiles. He was born on a farm in Cleveland county, began work at the age of nine at a store in Charlotte, and later helped organize Gastonia's Citizens National Bank. He had his work cut out for him at Textiles-Incorpoted. The first year the company lost $800,000, according to an account published in Textile Bulletin. The officers cut their salaries in half. Land around the mills was turned into gardens, and canning plants were set up to help tide workers through the slow period.

The yarn spinning mills had the toughest time surviving. But Threads fared much better, operating almost every workday through the Depression years and opening up sales offices throughout the country. This was a pattern that would be repeated over the years. Other parts of the textile industry would be mired in a slump, but Threads would remain

steady, due to its wide customer base. That helps smooth out the peaks and valleys in the business cycle.

Texiles-Incorporated was turned back to its stockholders at the beginning of World War II, and until going private in 1983, it never failed to pay a dividend.

Beginning in the 1950s, Textiles-Incorporated began a series of acquisitions in the Carolinas and elsewhere. Threads acquired Roxy Thread Company of New York in the early 1960s and later opened a small winding and quilling operation in Whitmire, South Carolina. Overseas expansion began with the purchase of Threads of Puerto Rico and the opening of a sales and distribution office in Sint-Niklaas, Belgium.

The name of the company was changed to Ti-Caro, Inc. (for Textiles-Incorporated of the Carolinas) in 1978, and two years later, it was listed on the New York Stock Exchange.

Management led a leveraged buyout in 1983, and Ti-Caro became a private company. The next few

Victory card room with view of modern roving frame.

years were challenging for the textile industry. Stiff competition from foreign imports forced the closing or sale of several Ti-Caro plants, including the Threads plant in Whitmire. Then, in 1986, an agreement was reached for Dixie Yarns of Chattanooga, Tennessee, to acquire all the stock of Ti-Caro and make it a wholly owned subsidiary.

It made Threads part of a larger corporation that was in an economic position to invest in the business. The other divisions of Dixie Yarns include Candlewick Yarns, Carriage Industries (a carpet manufacturer), Masland Carpets, the Dixie Yarn Group, and Caro-Knit.

The combined companies have 7,300 employees in California, Alabama, Georgia, Tennessee, the Carolinas, and Puerto Rico with sales of some $600 million annually.❑

Threads Finishing, dye department-modern package dye machinery.

Firestone Fibers & Textiles Co

*The new **Firestone** facility at Kings Mountain. Construction was completed in spring 1993.*

A quiet revolution took place at Firestone Fibers & Textiles Company in 1993.

The plant, which has operated in Gastonia since 1935, moved into a new building near Kings Mountain, completely revamped its production, and retrained its workers.

The changes will make Firestone at least 40 percent more productive per man-hour, and it has already resulted in better-trained, multi-skilled employees.

Company officials knew they had to replace the six-story, red-brick building constructed at the turn of the century and provide a more efficient working place. Valuable man-hours were wasted in the time it took to transport materials in between floors for the processes of twisting and weaving fiber into tire cord and industrial fabric.

But Firestone needed more than a new building; it needed a whole new way of operating. As a result, it began an extensive six-week training program for all employees and completely changed its organization.

Employees learn about teamwork, total quality control, problem solving, and safety, as well as process education. They are cross-trained to do all facets of the plant's three basic processes—ply twisting, cable twisting, and weaving. Before, the company had approximately 100 specific job classifications, such as ply twisting operator, weaver, or materials handler. The new process requires just two classifications: team leader and team member.

Raw materials are brought directly to three self-contained production areas, each with teams capable of completing the entire process of manufacturing tire cord. Such organization is easier in the new single-story, air-conditioned plant, which has 430,000 square feet.

"There's a tremendous bond when you work as a team," says Plant Manager Rowe Henderson. "Traditionally, Gastonia factories were very autocratic in terms of management style. There's been a total management turnover here since the mid-1980s. We try to use more employee participation."

The willingness of employees to learn new methods is why Firestone decided to keep a plant in Gaston County instead of build one elsewhere. Firestone offers an in-house learning center where employees can learn basic skills, work in a high school equivalency program, or acquire higher math skills. An open house introducing the classroom drew 60 participants. It is also open to retired Firestone employees. Gaston County has long had a high number of adults who lack basic skills.

The education is needed in order to help employees do statistical process control and problem solving in the production process. "The most substantial change has been accountability," says Henderson. "You're putting all the decision making to the most basic level." Employees have two missions: outstanding service to customers and high manufacturing efficiency. The latter involves not just production but also safety, cost-effectiveness, teamwork, and a commitment to quality. "Their only responsibility before was productivity," says Henderson.

The teamwork concept applies to salaried employees also. There are two business units, one at the new Kings Mountain plant and one at the old plant, where Firestone keeps its treating facility, lab, and warehouse. The company has a total of approximately 350 employees.

They produce up to 150,000 pounds per day of finished, treated fabric. This is the equivalent of $5 million in tires. The finished fabric is dipped at the treating facility with a coating that enables it to adhere to rubber.

Firestone first located in Gastonia in 1935 to open a large plant for converting cotton to tire cord fiber. It selected the former Loray Mill, a 550,000-square-foot building that was once the largest textile mill under one roof in the world. In the early days, Firestone spun its own yarn, operating a plant that employed up to 3,000 people.

In the 1950s, it began to replace cotton with nylon and polyester as the construction of tires changed to synthetic materials. Firestone began to rely on two sister plants in Hopewell, Virginia, and Woodstock, Ontario, that supplied it with polyester and nylon.

*The old **Firestone** tower is a landmark in Gastonia.*

*Original six-story, red-brick **Firestone** building.*

Together, the three plants make up the Fibers and Textiles Division of Firestone.

The Bridgestone Corporation, a worldwide Japanese company headquartered in Tokyo, purchased Firestone in 1988. Nashville-based Bridgestone/Firestone is the largest subsidiary of Bridgestone Corporation. It develops, manufactures, and markets Bridgestone, Firestone, Dayton, private brand and house brand tires, as well as a wide range of industrial and synthetic rubber goods.

Bridgestone/Firestone has 22 plants in North, Central, and South America. The Kings Mountain plant is the main supplier of tire cord and industrial fabrics for Bridgestone's operations in the Western Hemisphere.

Jaggy Anand is president of the Firestone Fibers and Textiles Division which includes Gastonia and Kings Mountain as well as plants in Hopewell, Virginia; and Woodstock, Ontario, Canada. Rowe Henderson is the plant manager for both Kings Mountain and Gastonia and Terry Swanner and Bill Lindquist are business managers for the plants respectively. The company has long been active in the United Way. An award given each year to the outgoing president of United Way is named for Harold Mercer, a former president of the Gastonia Firestone plant.

Firestone managers spent a year developing their new team approach in Gaston County. When the company hires new employees now, a panel made up of management and hourly workers interview applicants.

At the opening of the new $20 million plant near Kings Mountain, Bridgestone/Firestone CEO Masatoshi Ono had this to say: "Bridgestone/Firestone wants to have a work force second to none in the industry. That not only means hiring capable, experienced employees and paying them a competitive wage, but also providing thorough and continuous job training, career development opportunities, and support for the well-being of their families."❑

Textile Parts & Machine Co., Inc.

In the midst of the Depression, M.B. Stewart gave up a good job as an accountant at an oil company to run his own business. It was an opportunity he felt he couldn't pass up. His brother-in-law, Lamar Cloniger, had bought a small textile machine repair shop, and he needed Stewart to run it.

Stewart took over and, in the next half century, oversaw the expansion of Textile Parts & Machine Co. to a 22,000-square-foot facility with computerized machinery to produce precision parts.

His sons, David and John, joined the company in the 1960s. All of their lives have revolved around the textile industry. M.B. Stewart's father was a farmer in Cherokee County, South Carolina, who came to Gastonia to work as a fixer in a textile mill. His brother-in-law, Lamar Cloniger, ran a grocery store in what was then the Firestone mill village, and later invested in mills in York, South Carolina.

Textile Parts & Machine Co. started in a 1,800-square-foot building on May Street in west Gastonia with six employees. It was doubled in size in 1950 and has undergone several expansions since then, but still considers the employees as one of its greatest assets.

But the biggest change in the business has been in the precision and speed with which gears are made for machinery that produces yarn. The company started out finishing cast-tooth gears. The gears came from the foundry with the teeth cast in them, and Textile Parts & Machine Co. finished them with lathes, milling machines, and drill presses.

The gears were used in all phases of yarn machinery, from the picker that took cotton from bales to the finishing end that wrapped the yarn on cones.

By the 1960s, textile machinery was produced that operated at much higher speeds than it had earlier. The gears manufactured by Textile Parts & Machine Co. had to be made closer to specifications in order to run at higher speeds. There was another big change—steel began to replace iron in textile machine parts.

"Everybody wanted to produce more. The machines were set up to run faster, which was in our favor because they wore out more gears," remembers M.B. Stewart.

Textile companies that had relied on in-house machine shops found they no longer had the time or sophistication to finish their own parts, and they began to rely more heavily on companies like Textile Parts & Machine Co.

In 1967, Textile Parts & Machine Co. switched from manually run lathes to automatic machines that could turn out a set number of parts without resetting. Then, 10 years later, the company bought its first computerized machine, which enabled operators to punch in the specifications and turn out as many gears as was needed.

Today, Textile Parts & Machine Co. has 32 employees who run eight computerized lathes and one computerized milling center plus other metal working machines. It serves yarn manufacturers throughout the Southeast. In the past 15 years, it has begun manufacturing parts to metric measurements to

(L to R) John Stewart, M.B. Stewart, David Stewart

accommodate foreign-made machinery.

The company also manufactures parts made of nylon and fiber that are used to keep the noise down in machinery. It continues to improve its equipment to keep up with changes in the textile industry.

"My greatest satisfaction is being able to serve the customer with a quality product," says M.B. Stewart. "Henry Ford said, `It is not the employer who pays wages—he only handles the money. It's the customer who pays wages.'"❏

Textile Parts & Machines Co. has expanded to a 22,000 square-foot facility with computerized machinery.

Public Service Company of North Carolina, Inc.

PSNC corporate headquarters in Gastonia.

Public Service Company of North Carolina, Inc. (PSNC), headquartered in Gastonia, serves natural gas customers in some of the fastest growing areas of the state. PSNC's service territory includes 89 North Carolina cities and communities in 26 counties and spans from the Research Triangle area (Raleigh, Durham, and Chapel Hill) in the north central portion of the state; to the Concord, Statesville, Gastonia, and Forest City region in the Piedmont; to Asheville, Hendersonville, and Brevard in the west.

The company began operations in Gastonia in the mid-1930s when Founder Charles Branson Zeigler purchased the Gastonia and Suburban Gas Company. Gaston County was a strategic choice. Natural gas was needed to process cotton through every phase of its treatment at dozens of textile mills in the area. By the 1940s, the county had the highest concentration of textile mills of any place in the country.

In the beginning, the company grew through acquisitions. The Concord and Kannapolis Gas Company became part of the Gastonia and Suburban Gas Company in 1938, when the present company name, Public Service Company of North Carolina, Inc., was adopted. In 1939, the National Utilities

Company of North Carolina, Inc., a gas company operating in Statesville, was merged into PSNC. The Durham Gas Company, the Asheville Gas Company, and the Raleigh Gas Company were acquired in 1943.

In 1955, Charles Branson Zeigler became chairman and his son Branson E. Zeigler was elected president. Branson was later succeeded by his brother Charles E. Zeigler, Sr. as president and chairman. Today, Charles E. Zeigler, Jr. is chairman, president, and chief executive officer.

A number of milestones occurred in the 1960s. The customer count had more than quadrupled to 50,000 by 1961. The greater Research Triangle Park was beginning to boom. That region is now the home for 60 percent of the company's customers. A new corporate headquarters was completed in Gastonia in 1965. It is one of six offices currently located in Gaston County.

During the 1970s, PSNC began making plans to ensure a steady supply of natural gas for its ever-increasing number of customers. In 1976 the Charles Branson Zeigler Energy Center was dedicated. Situated on 70 acres between Raleigh and Cary, it houses a one billion-cubic-foot liquified natural gas storage facility and a one million-gallon propane-air storage facility.

By 1979, annual operating revenues exceeded $100 million and 725 employees served 135,000 cus-

tomers. During the 1980s, as a result of the company's focus on superior customer service and value, PSNC was selected from a field of 300 natural gas utilities operating in North America as one of the top-rated marketing utilities.

Because of North Carolina's positive economic climate and the strong demand for natural gas, PSNC's customer growth rate has been almost triple the national average for the past ten years. This rate of growth is expected to continue throughout the 1990s.

Today approximately 1,100 employees serve more than 270,000 customers from 21 area offices across the state. Where natural gas is available, PSNC provides gas to more than 60 percent of existing homes and businesses in its service territory.

As PSNC looks to the future, it is focused on expanding existing markets by providing superior customer service and value. The company is also seizing marketing opportunities presented by the development of new natural gas technologies in the areas of natural gas cooling and natural gas vehicles; and expanding its offerings to include intrastate pipeline services and interstate supply and capacity brokering.□

PSNC began operations in Gastonia in the mid-1930s in this office building. Natural gas was needed by the textile mills in the area.

AMP

*An array of **AMP** interconnection products and the tools to apply them.*

AMP is the world leader in the system interconnection business because it constantly finds ways to improve.

The company was founded on the premise that it could produce better electrical terminations than traditional methods used by the aircraft and ship-building industries. To replace soldering, AMP introduced the concept of connecting terminals to electrical wires by crimping. With this new method, the company became a prime supplier to companies that were filling the demands generated by World War II. After the war, the company redirected its business to commercial applications.

Based in Harrisburg, Pennsylvania, AMP has grown steadily ever since its founding in 1941. In addition to electrical and electronic connectors, it also provides fiber optic products, printed circuit boards and assemblies, networking products, and other highly engineered products and services. In 1993 the company recorded $3.45 billion in sales from operations in 36 countries.

As the company grew, it opened small plants near urban areas. Gaston County's pool of skilled labor first drew the multinational company to build a plant here in 1966.

AMP operations began in Gastonia with 12 employees making dies for metal stamping in a 12,500-square-foot shop on Northwest Boulevard in Bessemer City. Within a decade, the size of the original plant quadrupled to include manufacturing. Today five billion contacts a year are stamped and plated in the original Gastonia plant.

The company later opened a plating plant on Shannon-Bradley Road in South Gastonia and an assembly operation in Lowell. The three plants employ more than 800 people.

"This is where it all begins," says Gastonia plant manager Joe Waugh. "If we don't have metal, we can't make electrical contacts."

James Ramseur, a metal trade supervisor, was one of the first employees in Gastonia. Impressed by the AMP benefit package, he signed on. "It sounded too good to be true," recalls Ramseur, who left a tool and die company to join AMP.

During the past decade, the Gastonia operation has focused on streamlining production and eliminating downtime. In 1986, 39 presses could produce 180 million contacts per month. Today, just 22 presses produce almost three times as much—some 500 million contacts per month.

Most contacts are made from one metal, and plated with another. The ultimate use for a product determines the type of electroplating it receives. For example, when contacts are plated with 30 microinches of gold, they are suitable for use in extreme reliability applications such as Patriot missiles used by the U.S. military. For commercial use, 15 microinches of gold are plated contacts that go into personal computers. Tin plating is suitable for connections in items such as bathroom scales and washing machines.

To protect the environment and minimize costs, all electroplating is done at one plant. But AMP is integrating other manufacturing operations so that molding, stamping, and assembly can be done in a single facility. This allows employees at each plant to be cross-trained in multiple jobs and to see the entire process of putting the product together.

"We put the destiny of the product in the hands of the team," says Johnny Norton, manager of the plating plant. Quality is tightly controlled—the dimension of components are precise from three millionths to two hundred millionths of an inch depending on thickness specification.

Employees are always coming up with ways to improve processes. For example, thanks to employee-generated improvements, die replacements that used to take up to several hours are now completed in as little as 12 minutes. Advances like these are considered essential at AMP locations around the world, and Gastonia is no exception.❏

*The **AMP** assembly operation in Lowell, combined with two other area facilities, employ more than 800 people.*

JPS Converter & Industrial Corporation

The JPS Converter and Industrial Corp. plant in Stanley has a long history of innovation.

In the past 50 years, it has pioneered processes for manufacturing synthetic yarns, dying fibers, making orlon socks, and producing worsted wool yarn.

Before extensive automation, it employed up to 900 people. Now there are 370 employees, and the plant produces up to 450,000 pounds of synthetic yarn each week that ends up in apparel, home furnishings, automobiles, and other commercial uses.

Since 1988, when West-Point Pepperell bought out J.P. Stevens & Co., the company has been one of four corporations under JPS Textile Group, headquartered in Greenville, South Carolina.

The buildings that make up the Stanley plant went through several different owners before becoming part of JP Stevens and Co. in 1941. The oldest, the Lola Mill, was constructed in 1888 and operated as a yarn dye operation by Hubert M. Craig and his father, Robert Craig. Next to it was the Lola Gingham Mill, built in 1918 and owned by Katterman and Mitchell, a New Jersey company that operated a silk-weaving mill until 1939.

The Lola Gingham Mill stood idle until 1941, when it was purchased by a group headed by O. Max Gardner, a former governor of North Carolina. Several important developments took place under Gardner's leadership: The main part of the mill was renovated, an addition was built, and the production of spun rayon yarn began with 10,000 spinning spindles.

J.P. Stevens & Co. acquired the Lola Mill and Lola Gingham Mill in 1946 and soon introduced a new way to produce worsted yarn on machinery that had traditionally been used to produce cotton yarn. Before, such production was done on specially built machinery.

"It was a real breakthrough in the cost of producing worsted yarn," remembers former Plant Manager R.P. Sullivan, who joined the company as a management trainee in 1946 and retired as general manager in 1982.

There was another innovation in the 1950s: JPS was the first plant in the United States to produce yarns made from solution-dyed fiber. This produced a color-fast yarn that was especially good for draperies and other fabrics, because it prevented them from fading when exposed to sunlight.

The plant continued to grow. In 1962, an air-conditioned addition was constructed next to the old Lola Mill. This brought the total number of spindles to 43,000, making it one of the largest spinning operations in Gaston County. Working in con-

JPS Converter & Industrial Corporation, Stanley Plant, Stanley, N.C.

junction with DuPont, the plant developed a new process that stretched orlon under heat, breaking the fibers into different lengths to make yarn for a "stretchable" sock. They were far superior to the stretchable nylon socks that had previously been on the market.

"We could name our own price for the yarn at that time," remembers Charles A. Rhyne, who retired as plant manager in 1981 after 29 years with the company.

The plant was always flexible. "As the cotton market grew stronger, we had the ability to convert part of the spinning back and forth to cotton and rayon or synthetics," says Sullivan. In 1989, the plant converted its long staple operation to short staple. In 1992, an open-end spinning project was completed and will be expanded in March 1994. The plant's emphasis now is totally on synthetics, and it continues to supply outside customers and other JPS Weaving Mills with quality yarns.

The current plant manager is D.E. Eaker. JPS Converter and Industrial Corporation is headed by R.A. Muckenfuss, Director of manufacturing. Jerry Hunter is the President of JPS Textile Group. ❑

In 1963, J.P. Stevens celebrated its 150th anniversary. Pictured below is R.P. Sullivan, General Manager, John C. Fonville, Administrative Manager, James W. Cannon, Personnel Manager & Charles A. Rhyne, Plant manager. The four former J.P. Stevens Managers pictured below have a combined total of 145 years of service with J.P. Stevens & Co., Inc.

Smith Textile Apron Company

*D*an Gunter's life as a child revolved around the textile mills. His father was a superintendent at Burlington Industries. His mother was a production worker. From the time he was a teenager, Gunter did odd jobs in textile mills.

He founded Smith Textile Apron Company, Inc. in 1952, building on the tradition of the company his father-in-law had begun in 1944. Over the next few decades, Smith Textile Apron Company became the country's dominant producer of textile machinery used in cleaning and conveying cotton.

"Anything that has a steel pin in it we can make," says Gunter.

The company employs 45 people in a 36,000-square-foot facility on South U.S. Highway 321. It manufactures aprons with wooden, plastic, metal, or aluminum slats that are mounted on different types of belting. Although the bulk of Smith Textile Apron's customers are in the textile industry, the company also produces parts for bedding manufacturers, nonwoven plants (which make paper goods), and plants that produce products for the automotive industry such as dashboards and carpeting. Smith Textile Apron sells throughout the United States, as well as in Mexico and Canada.

Gunter got his start in the business in 1946, when he went to work for his father-in-law, Yates Smith, and Smith's partner Fred McFalls. Gunter had graduated from high school, served in the Air Force two years, and attended North Carolina State and Belmont Abbey before marrying DeDe Smith. His father-in-law put him to work in sales, making $50 a week.

"I had a good rapport with the textile companies," says Gunter. "I could talk to the mill owner, superintendents, overseers or production workers."

A few years after Gunter joined the company, he purchased McFalls' 40 percent interest. After Yates Smith died in 1952, Gunter, as surviving partner, ran the business for a year. At this time, Mrs. Smith decided to sell her interest to a group of outsiders. Once this decision to sell was made, Gunter formed his own business from scratch. As surviving partner, he had the option of incorporating the name Smith Textile Apron Company, which he did.

First he had to scrounge for machinery. He bought used equipment for $1,400 from a businessman in Blacksburg, South Carolina, and set about rebuilding it, working at night and on weekends.

"When I first went into business, I was doing all the traveling," Gunter remembers. "I would leave on a Sunday afternoon and drive to Georgia, and Alabama, and be gone two or three weeks. When I got back home, I had to do pricing of products and see that they were invoiced. It seemed like every time I returned, my boy had grown several inches."

He started out with six employees. Hourly wages ranged from 75 cents to $1.10. One, Vera Robertson, was a secretary at the company for 28 years.

The company's first office was a small building on West Second Street. After about a year, Gunter built a new 5,000-square-foot facility on North U.S. Highway 321. The building was partially destroyed by a fire in 1966, but it never halted business. The fire

*The present **Smith Textile Apron Company** building, built in 1973.*

*The old **Smith Textile Apron Company** building, built in 1955.*

in charge of payroll, joined Smith Textile Apron in 1963.

General Manager David Lawson got his first job at age 18 in 1973. He started as a production worker. "You're never doing the same thing," says Lawson. "I enjoy the gratification of taking the order, watching the product start from a diagram, and seeing it through to a finished product."

The textile industry has eliminated some of the equipment that once required Smith Textile Apron products. As a result, the company has diversified, manufacturing components for textile machinery.

"We're always changing the product line," says Lawson, "and we'll be changing it in years to come. If we didn't do that, we would have been out of business a long time ago."❑

was believed to have been caused by a gas heater igniting dust.

Two expansions doubled the size of the building. By the early 1970s, it was clear Smith Textile Apron needed more space. It moved to its present location in 1973. In the 1980s, an additional 10,000-square-foot building was constructed for the woodworking plant, which manufactures slats and other wooden items.

Visitors to Smith Textile Apron often frequent the Wolfpack Den, a conference room full of North Carolina State athletics memorabilia, including pictures from the Wolfpack's NCAA championships. Gunter himself was a high school sports star, lettering in football, baseball, and basketball.

Besides being an avid Wolfpack fan, Gunter has also been active in politics and civic organizations. He served four years on the Gastonia City Council and was elected mayor in 1963. He served for eight years each on the Board

of Governors for the University of North Carolina system and the Board of Trustees for North Carolina State University.

Twice he was elected Boss of the Year by the National Secretaries Association International. Several employees have been with the company many years. Judy Jenkins, who is

*Left, David Lawson, general manager; right, Dan Gunter, founder of **Smith Textile Apron Company, Inc.***

Southern Specialty Printing

Gastonia had a mission after World War II: To attract other kinds of industry to the thriving textile community. City leaders formed the Gastonia Industrial Diversification Commission, headed by Allen Smith. The first company recruited by the commission was Southern Paper Industries, Inc.

It turned out to be a good match. Founder Allen Perry Folk established a company in May of 1947 that manufactured business forms and tags for all kinds of industries.

Folk had worked in the printing and tag manufacturing business in St. Louis and Atlanta when Gastonia business leaders contacted him about opening a company here. Folk agreed to lease one of four buildings that had been constructed by the Gastonia Industrial Realty Corp., which worked with the Industrial Diversification Commission.

Today, the president and principal stockholder is Albert Richard "Bud" Morris, who began his career with the company as an office clerk in June of 1948. After having just completed a degree in commerce, Bud approached Folk about joining the company. Bud had spent the previous 30 months studying at the University of North Carolina at Chapel Hill while recovering from war injuries received during the Battle of the Bulge in Europe.

There was an instant rapport between Bud and Folk. This close business relationship lasted 5 years, until Folk retired. At that time, there were 4 companies operating under Folk's leadership: National Tag and Ticket, which made custom tags and tickets; Southern Paper Industries, Inc., which was a retailer and wholesaler of paper products; Standard Business Forms, which made carbon-interleaved forms; and Folgo Enterprises, which designed

and made equipment to produce custom printing products. Folgo and National Tag were absorbed by Southern Paper Industries, Inc. (the name was later changed to Southern Specialty Printing, Inc. in 1977), and Standard Business Forms was sold to a relative of Folk. In 1953, Folk retired.

The company underwent several important transitions in the 1950s. After Folk left, Sales Manager H. Cabel Jordan served as president for close to two years. He then returned to sales, and Albert Richard Rankin, Morris's uncle, became president, a job he held until 1975, when Bud, who had been vice president and treasurer, took over.

In 1957, the company did away with its sales force and began a practice it continues today—no direct sales—operating through more than 600 distributors, who sell to the direct consumer and then place the orders with Southern Specialty Printing, Inc. for manufacturing.

The company's emphasis is on specialty printing jobs. This can range from a 17-part form that follows a sofa through the manufacturing process, to

a simple, plain tag. It can handle small "stopgap" jobs, an ability that has given the company an edge during slower economic times.

Southern Specialty Printing, Inc. purchased the two buildings it occupied in the 1950s. They were joined and cover about 30,000-square-feet. They currently employ 43 people, about half the staff it required before extensive automation. Some of the machinery will print, perforate, diecut, punch holes, reinforce the holes and add metal eyelets to tags.

Other key people in the business are R. Steve Forrest, Executive Vice President, who joined the company in 1965, and Glenda J. Arndt, Vice President/Secretary/Assistant Treasurer, who has been there since 1957. Glenda Huffstetler Hardee, Assistant Secretary, joined the company in 1973. Michael R. Pasour, Customer Relations and Estimator, was employed in 1988, and Caroline Moore Hildenbrand was employed in 1992. James W. McAbee, Plant Superintendent, started out with the company as a pressman in 1972.❑

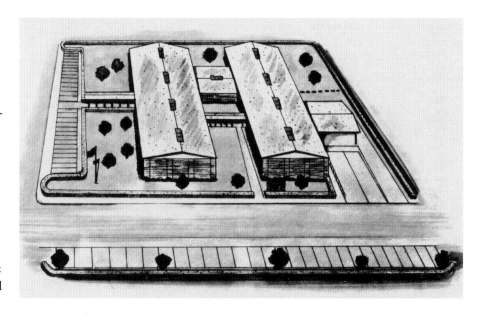

Ithaca Industries

Ithaca Industries is one of the largest purchaser of spun yarns in the United States. So it made sense for the Wilkesboro, North Carolina-based company to open a plant in Gaston County, the center of the textile industry's yarn-spinning operations.

The plant opened in 1978 and now takes in 200,000 square feet on Tulip Drive in northwest Gastonia. It started with a staff of 300 and has grown to 700.

Ithaca Industry's Gastonia operation makes the fabric for men's and boys' briefs and T-shirts and women's cotton panties. Its fabric is shipped to sewing plants in eastern North Carolina and Georgia.

The company is constantly updating its equipment. Some of its knitting machines can operate at up to 1,000 revolutions per minute.

Plant Manager James Hall serves on the city's Citizen Advisory Committee for water and sewer improvement. Ithaca is the city's biggest industrial water user.

The company is a strong supporter of the United Way and is also involved with the Boy Scouts, the Schiele Museum, the Gastonia Little Theater, and a drug prevention program sponsored by the police department.

The plant's parent corporation, Ithaca Industries, was founded in 1948 in Ithaca, New York, as a manufacturer of women's underwear. In the late 1960s, Ithaca closed its New York facilities and relocated its corporate headquarters to Wilkesboro, North Carolina. The company,

originally family-owned, was purchased in a leveraged buy out by an investor group, which included current management, in 1983.

Shortly after its founding, Ithaca focused primarily on business with J.C Penney and became its major supplier of private label women's underwear. In 1969, Ithaca began to produce hosiery. In 1976, Ithaca added men's and boys' underwear to its product line and within a couple of years opened the Gastonia plant to supply that division with fabric.

The Gastonia operation knits, dyes, or bleaches virtually all of the fabric used in the manufacture of men's and boys' underwear and outerwear. The plant has a fully automated system of production control. The system integrates the processes of order entry and production scheduling, and moves goods through the production process while tracking material, overhead, and labor costs.

Ithaca has long been an industry leader in product innovation. It con-

structed the first successful control top pantyhose. The company also holds a patent on the design for its total support pantyhose.

Ithaca is the largest domestic manufacturer of women's panties and the largest manufacturer of women's private label hosiery. The company has many recognizable names such as Evan Picone, Hang Ten, Lightning Bolt, Lady Manhatten, Perry Ellis, and many more. It has the dominant private label market share, the broadest array of products and styles, and the largest customer base (1,500) in America in each of its hosiery, men's and boys' underwear, and women's and girls' underwear product lines. Its customers include Banana Republic, The Gap, K-Mart, The Limited, Nike, J.C. Penney, Saks Fifth Avenue, Wal-Mart, Ralph Lauren (Polo), and many others.◻

The Ithaca Industries Gaston Plant opened in 1978 and now takes in 200,000 square feet.

John Bisanar, Inc.

John Bisanar started his electrical contracting business with one dollar, a willingness to moonlight after his regular job, and an office in his home garage.

The year was 1937, and Bisanar was an electrician at the giant Firestone Fibers & Textiles plant in Gastonia. He spent a decade running his business on the side before breaking off to make John Bisanar, Inc. a full-time electrical contractor.

In the almost 60 years it has been in business, John Bisanar, Inc. has done work for dozens of textile mills, retail establishments, banks, churches, and homes.

Bisanar sold the company to long-time employees James Robinson and Catharine (Kitty) Holland in 1980. But he still serves as a consultant.

The company has thousands of clients throughout the Southeast and keeps a staff of between 30 and 45 people. Its primary focus is on water and wastewater construction. The work John Bisanar, Inc. did at the Lincoln County Water Treatment Plant, which involved high-tech digital controls, was featured in *Professional Engineer Digest* in 1991.

Founder John Bisanar grew up in Lincoln County, the son of a farmer.

By high school, he was already getting experience in electrical work by helping the school system install 32-volt generators. He worked odd jobs for several years before enrolling in a four-month program at Coyne Electrical School in Chicago. After returning to Gastonia, he was hired by the Manville-Jenckes textile company, first to work at the High Shoals plant, and then at the company's Gastonia plant, which was later bought by Firestone.

Bisanar was serving as a plant electrician when a violent strike broke out in 1929. The company paid him half-time to sleep in the switchboard room during the disturbance, and he remembers being frightened when he discovered one worker with a sawed-off shotgun.

Bisanar eventually received his electrical license and began doing work on the side, out of his home.

"We'd go out at four o'clock and by eight o'clock we'd have a four-room house wired," recalls Bisanar.

Plagued by respiratory problems caused by dust in the mill, Bisanar left Firestone in 1948 and began full-time electrical contracting from an office at 207 South Firestone Street. He had four full-time and two part-time

John Bisanar, founder of John Bisanar, Inc.

employees, paid from 90 cents to $1.20 an hour. His brother James joined the company in 1951, and its name was changed to J & J Electric Service.

A turning point for the company came when it contracted with Akers Motor Lines to do the electrical wiring for a warehouse in 1949. Founded in 1933, Akers was at that time one of the largest trucking companies in the country. The initial contract with Akers led to numerous other jobs, from Georgia to Pennsylvania.

Catharine (Kitty) Holland joined the company in 1964 as bookkeeper. She is now secretary-treasurer. James Robinson joined the company in 1971 after being discharged from the Navy. He is president.

In 1977, J & J Electric was divided into two companies—John Bisanar, Inc. and Jim Bisanar Heating & Air Conditioning. John Bisanar, Inc. moved to its present location at 326 South Avon Street. In the previous years, the company had occupied offices on West Franklin and at Akers Center.

Bisanar's five grandsons were trained as electricians, and six former employees trained by Bisanar went on to form their own electrical contracting businesses.❑

Akers Shopping Center was the first shopping center in Gaston County. John Bisanar, Inc. wired every store in the center and installed the Widelite 1000 Watt Mercury parking lot lighting. The center was featured in national electrical magazines.

W.D. Lee & Company Inc.

Mr. W.D. Lee

Mrs. Mary Myers Lee

*T*he late William Doyle Lee was no stranger to hard work. At age 10 he took his first job at a textile mill in Gastonia.

That was in 1920. In the following decades, Mr. W.D. Lee worked for companies like Firestone, Threads, and CDA. He learned how to install and repair textile machinery, and began doing some work on his own.

By 1954, he felt he had enough work to organize his own business. He worked out of his home for a year and a half, then opened an 8,000-square-foot machine shop at 217 Ransom Street. His wife, Mary Myers Lee, served as bookkeeper and office manager until her retirement in 1980.

W.D. Lee & Company, Inc. built a reputation for producing precision machine parts within a short turnaround time. Although for many years it served the textile industry exclusively, it now produces machine parts for a wide range of industries.

W.D. Lee's son, Jerry Lee, is now president. He joined the company after graduating from Gastonia High School and serving four years in the Navy. Jerry's sons, David and Dennis Lee, are vice presidents, and his daughter, Karen Rhyne, is secretary and treasurer of the company.

The business expanded in 1968, building a shop on Trakas Boulevard, just off West Franklin. It now has more than 22,000 square feet and employs 26 people.

The company uses eight computerized lathes and six computerized milling centers. It also has a new computerized machine that does both turning and milling. While manual lathes move at 20 inches a minute, the new machinery moves at 1,100 inches a minute. "It's lightning fast, and it's real easy to program," says Dennis Lee, who studied computer science at Appalachian State University before joining the family business. The computerized machinery also allows operators to make parts that are within one ten-thousandth of an inch to specifications.

About a third of W.D. Lee & Company's work is for the textile business. The rest is for a wide variety of industries. Among its products are molds for making styrofoam used for shipping products, parts for woodworking machinery, gears and shafts for any type of machinery, and molds for plastic supplies.

"W.D. Lee was good with machinery," says his son Jerry, "and he also had a knack for dealing with employees and customers." W.D. Lee's parents moved to Gastonia around the turn of the century to work in the mills. They had made a living building chairs in Andrews, North Carolina, a mountain community.

W.D. Lee was active in the company he founded until the year before he died, in 1990.❑

Alala Mullen Holland & Cooper, P.A.

J. Mack Holland

James Mullen

A shortage of office space in post-World War II Gastonia propelled J. Mack Holland and James "Moon" Mullen into a partnership that has lasted more than 40 years.

The pair were World War II veterans, graduates of Duke Law School, starting practices in the late 1940s. Mack Holland rented space in a three-room suite at the Commercial Building from a cotton broker. When the cotton broker moved elsewhere, he invited James Mullen to share space.

"We continued to practice by ourselves but were able to back each other up if one was out of town or had a conflict," recalls Holland, a former president of the North Carolina Bar Association.

Four years of sharing an office and secretary convinced Holland the two would make a good team. Mullen's expertise was in civil trial work, and Holland's specialty was corporate and business law.

The pairing worked, and Holland and Mullen's partnership eventually evolved into today's firm: Alala Mullen Holland & Cooper, P.A.

Now one of the largest firms in the Charlotte area, its focus is civil law

matters, with particular expertise in banking, bankruptcy and reorganization, creditors' rights, employment discrimination, estate planning and administration, hospital and health care, mergers and acquisitions, negligence and personal injury, insurance, real estate, taxation, and a wide range of other business matters. The firm practices in all courts.

Over the years, it has been in five different locations in or near downtown. Since 1990, the firm has been in a Georgian Revival style house built in 1928 in York Chester, one of the city's oldest neighborhoods, and a registered historic district. The building underwent extensive expansion and renovations in 1988, adding a dramatic atrium and large offices with fireplaces and conference areas.

Holland still keeps limited office hours, and Mullen is retired. But their influence is still felt. The firm has a long tradition of being active in the Gaston County and North Carolina bar associations.

Its partners have included a North Carolina Bar Association president, a Gaston County Bar Association president, three members of the Board of

Governors of the North Carolina Bar Association, a member of the North Carolina Board of Law Examiners, and a Federal District Court judge (Graham Mullen, son of a founder).

Long before it was a requirement for attorneys to attend continuing education programs, Mullen and Holland insisted on it. The result is a highly qualified firm with all members educated in the latest developments in law. "Mack Holland and Moon Mullen are two of the finest lawyers in this state. They set high standards for us, and are directly responsible for the current high calibre of the firm," says Managing Partner Langdon Cooper, who is certified by state and national boards in consumer and business bankruptcy law. Another firm member, John H. Griffing, is a certified public accountant and certified by the state board in estate planning. (Board certification is a recent development in law, and lawyers applying for certification must do extensive preparation and complete rigorous written exams.)

The firm has the highest rating (a-v) given by Martindale-Hubbell, the national publication that rates attorneys, and four of the firm's partners also have an individual a-v rating.

When he thinks back on his career, Holland remembers helping people. "You get a lot of satisfaction out of being able to solve people's problems," he says. Back when the firm handled more criminal work, it defended a Bessemer City woman accused of murdering her husband. The firm received criticism for taking the case, but it turned out that the woman's husband was abusive and had threatened to kill the couple's oldest daughter. The woman was acquitted. In another case, a banker in Mount Holly was embezzling a homeowner's insurance premiums, and the homeowner's house burned down. In a hotly contested trial, a jury found in favor of the homeowner, who was represented by Mullen and Holland's firm.

Mullen built a statewide reputation as a skilled and successful litigator, while Holland built a statewide reputation as a corporate lawyer, representing Textiles, Inc., N.C. Public Service Co., Citizens National Bank (now part of Branch Banking & Trust), Gaston Memorial Hospital, and Rauch Industries, among others. He was city attorney for 16 years.

"They all have been very responsive to our needs. If we have an emergency, we tell them, and they respond quickly," says Alex Hall, president of the western region of Branch Banking & Trust Company. BB&T has been a client for 40 years.

The firm is also recognized in the legal profession. In a 1990 court order involving a resort property at Lake Lure, Judge Marvin R. Wooten, senior U.S. bankruptcy judge, wrote about Langdon Cooper, a Duke University UNC-Chapel Hill graduate who appeared in the United States Supreme Court in 1992, "Mr. Cooper is among the best and finest of the . . . attorneys serving and appearing in this court . . . He has served as counsel for trustees, debtors and creditors in some of the largest of the bankruptcy cases in the Western District, and his record of successfully recovering assets for creditors ... is well known."

Besides Cooper, the other senior members of the firm include: Joseph B. Alala, Jr., an honors UNC-Chapel Hill graduate, also a certified public accountant and author of numerous manuscripts on local, state, and federal taxation. He is a frequent lecturer in the continuing legal education program of the North Carolina Bar Association and the American and North Carolina Institute of CPAs. He

specializes in tax and business matters, and is widely known throughout North Carolina for his thorough and creative business planning. Notes Managing Partner Cooper: "Joe joined our firm in 1991 to manage our corporate and tax departments. He is one of the elite lawyers in North Carolina—strictly a number one draft choice."

R. T. Wilder, Jr., a magna cum laude graduate of Wake Forest University and Duke University Law School, who also served as an assistant U.S. attorney in the Western District of North Carolina and was elected to the American Board of Trial Advocates in 1990, an honor reserved for only the best litigators. He specializes in civil litigation and hospital and health care law. He also lectures in continuing legal education programs.

H. Randolph Sumner, a UNC-Chapel Hill and Wake Forest graduate who practices primarily in the areas of civil litigation, insurance defense, Social Security, and Workers' Compensation claims. He lectures and writes extensively in his areas of expertise. He has received numerous awards for his pro bono work, to which he has devoted hundreds of hours of free legal services.

Nancy Borders Paschall, a cum laude Wake Forest graduate who received numerous honors as a student at Wake Forest University Law School and practices primarily in the areas of civil and bankruptcy litiga-

tion. Paschall is very active in civic matters, currently serving as president of the Gaston County Red Cross.

Mark E. Shelley, a Davidson College and Wake Forest graduate who also obtained an LL.M. degree in tax from the University of Florida School of Law. He practices primarily in the area of business and tax law, serves as an instructor for the American Institute of Certified Public Accountants, and is the legal instructor for Gaston College's Small Business Center.

Other attorneys in the firm are Jane Foy Painter, J. Reid McGraw, Jr., Elizabeth Neisler Sumner, J. Mark Heavner, James H. Price, Jesse V. Bone, Jr., and Blake W. Hassan.

Members of the firm are involved in dozens of civic and church organizations, frequently serving in leadership roles. Since 1989, at least one lawyer in the firm has been been awarded a North Carolina Bar Association Volunteer Service Award each year. The Volunteer Service Award is given only to those lawyers who provide substantial amounts of free legal services to people who cannot afford to pay.☐

Alala Mullen Holland & Cooper is located in this beautiful Georgian Revival style house in one of the city's oldest neighborhoods.

Rauch Industries

The country's oldest producer of glass and unbreakable Christmas tree ornaments got its start in 1952 in Bessemer City.

But Rauch Industries didn't begin directly in Christmas ornaments. At first, Rauch bought yarn from local textile mills and wound it on paper cylinders for such uses as crochet thread, kite and wrapping cord. The company hit upon the idea of Christmas ornaments by chance. The paper cylinders covered with colorful yarn resembled ornaments. Why not, employees reasoned, take a styrofoam ball and give it a colored covering to make a decoration? Eventually the company developed and patented the satin Christmas ornaments that became its main line.

Today, Rauch does $50 million in sales and produces more than a million ornaments a day. Its acquisitions

have moved the company into other seasonal items, including glass ornaments, garland, icicles, aerosols, and Christmas stockings and tree skirts.

In 1990, Rauch Industries received the Entrepreneur of the Year Award from the state of North Carolina, honored for developing a product that had previously been dominated by imports.

It all began with six employees in 5,000 square feet of leased space in an old mill. Founder Marshall Rauch, who attended Duke University, took out a $3,500 mortgage on his house to open up shop. By 1956, Rauch had sales of $287,000. The company eventually expanded to include the remaining 35,000 feet of the Bessemer City mill, and in 1976, it built a new 230,000-square-foot plant on U.S. Highway 321 south of Gastonia. The company also acquired two properties from Burlington Industries—a 60,000-square-foot plant in Gastonia and a 660,000-square-foot plant in Cramerton.

Expansion continues today. A 200,000-square-foot warehouse scheduled for completion in 1994 will allow the company to operate more efficiently. Although the company manufactures 12 months a year, it ships out during just 3 months—August, September, and October. Additional warehouse space will allow the company to increase production and store ornaments until shipping season. The company has also added 10,000 square feet to its corporate offices.

The original satin-wrapped ornament, a portion of over a million ornaments produced each day.

There have been other changes besides expansion. In the 1980s, the satin ornaments division became almost fully automated, from molding to winding. Satin ornaments are molded from expandable polystyrene and wound with acetate or polyester yarn, which gives the ornaments a satin appearance.

"We feel we have the most modern and state-of-the-art equipment for manufacturing satin ornaments," says Rauch.

Now Rauch Industries is in the process of further automating its glass ornament manufacturing.

The company has made two major acquisitions in recent years. In 1984, Rauch acquired the Franke division of New Jersey-based Essex Chemical, a manufacturer of glass ornaments, icicles, garland, and Christmas aerosols. It closed the company's operations in Rhode Island and Missouri and

Screen-decorated glass ornaments enhance the company's Victoria line. Ornaments are also hand decorated with braids and other trim.

brought them to Gastonia. Then, in 1993, it acquired Holiday Products, a Rhode Island manufacturer of Christmas tree stockings, tree skirts, Santa Claus suits, and HoHo hats. Rauch closed the Rhode Island operation but kept plants in El Paso, Texas, and Ciudad Juarez, Mexico.

"The acquisitions allowed us to have a broader line of products we were competitive in," says Rauch.

Rauch Industries displays in major showrooms in Atlanta and New York, as well as 10 others operated by sales representatives all over the United States. Its 2,000 customers come under three market segments: mass merchants, such as Wal-Mart, Target,

Eckard's, and others; better department stores and gift shops; and the advertising specialty and premium trade.

The market has changed substantially over the years as large chains have acquired smaller ones and retail stores have consolidated.

Rauch Industries went public in 1983 and was listed on NASDAQ. In 1993, it switched to the American Stock Exchange. Although Rauch Industries is a publicly traded company, the founding family is still heavily involved in the business. Marshall Rauch is chairman of the board, president, and chief executive officer. His sons Marc F. Rauch and Peter D. Rauch and daughter Ingrid Rauch Sturm are all senior vice presidents of the company. Longtime employee Donald G. Walser is executive vice president and treasurer of the company.

The company averages 800 employees but goes up to as many as 1,200 at the peak of production. All employees receive stock through the Employee Stock Ownership Plan after one year of employment. In 1992, Rauch Industries was recognized by the state for its efforts to hire and promote women and minorities, receiving the North

Crochet thread was the company's first product. The Pyramid logo still appears on packaging today.

Carolina Human Relations Commission, Business and Industry Award for its commitment to excellence in human, economic, and educational development for its employees and the community.

Company employees have long been active in a wide range of community activities, including the YMCA, Salvation Army, Rotary, and others. Founder Marshall Rauch, besides his civic involvement, was a state senator for 24 years and is now chairman of the Budget and Finance Committee of the University of North Carolina Board of Governors.❑

"The Twelve Days of Christmas" is a top seller today for the company's MAGIC Division.

Sou-Tex Plant, Hoechst Celanese Corporation

By remaining actively committed to making quality products for customers, maintaining a safe workplace, and being a responsible corporate citizen, Hoechst Celanese and the Sou-Tex Plant have earned a reputation as a progressive economic and environmental partner with Gaston County.

The Sou-Tex Plant occupies a 37-acre tract in Mount Holly, in the heart of the southeast's textile producing region. It was founded in 1953 by a Pittsburgh businessman, H.M. Thompson, Jr., who settled in Mount Holly and named the Sou-Tex Chemical Company Inc. by combining the first three letters of "south" and "textiles."

The formula of the company's first major product had been developed by the 164-year-old Frankfurt dyestuff firm of Cassella Farbwerke Mainkur AG. Cassella provided both products and technical know-how to Sou-Tex, helping the tiny company survive and grow in the harshly competitive textile supplies industry.

In 1958, the firm had five employees, a product line of about ten dyestuffs and textile auxiliaries, and annual sales of $150,000. The first building, a production plant, was a former electrical substation from which the transformers had been removed and replaced with three small kettles.

The relationship between Cassella and Sou-Tex grew stronger in 1958, when the Frankfurt firm bought a minority interest in the little American company. The product line expanded and sulfur dyes for the cotton textile industry became big products.

More growth came with its acquisition by American Hoechst Corporation in 1973. Farbwerke Hoechst in Frankfurt had already become a part owner as the result of obtaining a majority of Cassella shares in 1969, acquiring Sou-Tex shares in the process. Two years later, it purchased Thompson's larger holdings in Sou-Tex.

American Hoechst's acquisition of the Sou-Tex Chemical Company evoked mixed feelings. A family feeling and informal intimacy had developed that comes from being in a small organization in a pleasant community. Employees soon realized they had the best of two worlds. Being able to tap into the vast financial and technological resources of one of the largest chemical companies in the world, brought them more economic growth and social benefits than would otherwise be imaginable. In the five years following the acquisition, employment grew to 100 and the value of Sou-Tex production more than doubled. In the process, Sou-Tex weathered an economic recession, discontinued sulfur

Hoechst Celanese logo originated from the clocktower & pedestrian bridge, which form the letter "h", & are striking architectural features of the Hoechst administrative headquarters erected in Frankfurt in 1924. The complex of buildings were designed by Peter Behrens, the leading German industrial architect of the early 20th century.

dye products, introduced new dyestuffs and production of plastic resins used as binding agents in inks, plastic laminates, can coatings, and adhesives. In addition, it brought on-stream a new $4.5 million "universal" plant—at the time, the largest capital expansion in Sou-Tex history.

The new plant doubled the capacity to manufacture numerous chemicals used by textile, agricultural, petroleum and other industries. It also positioned the plant to produce chemicals that were tailor-made for the American market and to pursue new areas, including basic surfactants formerly imported for sale to cosmetic and toiletries manufacturers.

The products included detergent raw materials, optical brighteners, fiber-preparation chemicals, softeners, dyeing assistants and bleaching agents, emulsifiers for the plant-protection industry, basic materials for anti-corrosive lubricants for metalworking, and multi-functional additives used in oil-well drilling.[1]

When American Hoechst merged with Celanese Corporation in 1987, the Sou-Tex Plant became part of the newly formed Hoechst Celanese Corporation, a multi-billion dollar

The **Hoechst Sou-Tex Plant** began operation in 1953 using this former electrical substation for blending and storage of dyestuffs and textile auxiliaries.

corporation, and a worldwide leader in chemicals, fibers and film, advanced materials and technologies, and the life sciences. It is the largest and fastest-growing member of the Hoechst Group, which operates 250 companies in about 120 nations.

The plant's strong ties to the textile industry continue today. It is the hub for blending, storage, and distribution of the Remazol® line of high-quality liquid fiber-reactive dyes for cotton, rayon, and blended textiles.

The Mount Holly facility currently produces more than 300 different specialty chemicals used in a variety of applications, including dyes and textile finishing agents, soaps, detergents and personal care products. Sou-Tex also produces DEET, the most widely used insect repellent ingredient in the world. DEET helps protect people from insect-borne diseases such as Lyme disease and Rocky Mountain spotted fever.

In 1993, construction began on a new building to increase the plant's dye manufacturing capability. Construction was also completed on a state-of-the-art wastewater treatment facility, which combines sophisticated high-tech computerized controls with environmentally friendly bacteria which naturally destroy waste prod-

ucts from the processes. Together, these two projects represent more than an $8 million investment.

The plant contributes to the local economy by spending more than $700,000 annually in Mount Holly, $2.5 million in Gaston County and, including payroll, $15 million in North Carolina.

The impact on the local community goes beyond dollars and cents. Many Sou-Tex employees serve on the plant's Fire and Emergency Safety Team (FEST). Their skills and knowledge make many of them highly valued members of local volunteer fire departments and rescue squads.

Concern for safety at Sou-Tex extends to the environment as well. The plant's continual improvement process is geared to eliminating the risk of accident and injury on the job and to ensuring that products and manufacturing processes are handled safely and in full compliance with environmental regulations.

As a member of the Chemical Manufacturers Association, Hoechst Celanese is an active participant in the group's Responsible Care™ initiative. This program is designed to address

*Aerial view of the **Hoechst Celanese Sou-Tex Plant**, which occupies a 37-acre site in Mount Holly.*

environmental and safety matters in communities in which Hoechst Celanese facilities operate.

The Sou-Tex Plant's 13-member community panel helps inform local citizens about the plant's operation and mission. The panel, which meets monthly, comprises a cross-section of the community.

Hoechst Celanese recognizes that being a good neighbor means going the extra step and being involved. The employees embody that spirit.

The name may not be a household word and might be hard to prounounce. But when some of America's best known companies look for new ways to improve their products, Hoechst Celanese is often the name that comes up first. Because when it's helping to make recycled plastic bottles for soft drink manufacturers, stretch yarn to make jeans more comfortable, or insulation for warmer sleeping bags for The North Face, Hoechst Celanese takes innovation and teamwork very seriously.

So when the name comes up, just say "Herkst Sel-a-neez."❑

*The first plant of the **Sou-Tex Chemical Company, Inc.**, destined to grow into the multibillion-dollar **Hoechst Celanese Corporation.***

1Edward Van Vlaanderen, Pronounced Success, America and Hoechst 1953-1978, K.A.S. Graphics Inc., 1979

First United Insurance Group, Inc.

Being professional, being the best, and always maintaining the highest standard of professional ethics was the philosophy and basis on which Ernest Petrey built his Insurance Agency that has led to the resulting loyalty of today's 8,500 clients.

Ernest's son, Harry Petrey, operates the Agency today from two turn of the century houses on East Third Avenue. Representing 15 major insurance carriers, as well as over 40 specialty markets, the 11 professionals and staff of 16 licensed associates have the knowledge and experience to provide the entire spectrum of insurance products and services required by its clients.

Ernest Petrey entered the insurance business in 1934 after graduation from the University of Tennessee. He worked for several companies before joining Liberty Mutual as Territorial Manager for North Carolina, Virginia, and Tennessee. In 1939, he joined his older brother Harry Lee Petrey, representing the Central Mutual Insurance Company.

In 1944, Petrey began service in the U.S. Navy. After the war, he returned to Gastonia, joining the firm of Watson Insurance in 1945. In 1954, Petrey started his own Agency, Ernest Petrey Insurance. He was, at the time, the only insurance professional in Gastonia with a college degree and industry training. His training and experience truly set him apart from his competition.

Harry Petrey began managing the Agency upon his father's death in 1974. A graduate of North Carolina State University, Petrey had previously been employed by the Jefferson Standard Life Insurance Company before heading the family firm. He was ably assisted by the firm's long term employees, as well as his mother,

Kathryn Peabody. Petrey's uncle, Harry L., joined the Agency in 1977. The transition from father to son management continued to emphasize the professional and ethical standards, providing for continuing growth.

In 1983, expansion began with the acquisition of the Kincaid Smith Insurance Agency in Bessemer City. Growth continued in 1984 when the company merged with two Gastonia firms, Anthony Adams Insurance Agency and The Terry Insurance Agency, forming the First United Insurance Group.

The company's principles are Harry Petrey, president, and John Land, executive vice president for finance and administration. Working in their respective fields of insurance and internal management, the combination works rather well.

First United continues to grow and prosper, selling more than $10 million in premium volume in its servicing area, about 70 percent being commercial coverage. In 1991, Petrey and Land expanded their operations to include management of an additional agency in the Charlotte-Mecklenburg market-

ing area. Other similar opportunities for future expansion are anticipated.

The initial philosophy of being professional, striving for the best, and the highest standards of professional ethics continue to be the cornerstone of the Agency's principals and goals, today and for the future.

Gaston Electric has been a customer for 30 years. "My father started Gaston Electric, and he did business with Harry's father; it just carried over," says owner Jerry Fogle. "I've had people try quoting other policies. When you add 30 years of service, you can't beat First United."❏

Ernest Q. Petrey, founder; Jean D. Hileman, retired secretary of the firm. 1960

Hillhaven Healthcare Of Gastonia

*F*ew nursing homes provide as wide a range of services as Hillhaven Healthcare of Gastonia. The 118-bed facility offers rehabilitative services (physical, occupational, and speech therapies), hospice, respite care, restorative nursing, short- and long-term care services—all provided from a wholistic team approach.

"People come here because they have specific needs," says Administrator Bob Goon. "We help to aid in the recovery from illness or injury, and from here the residents begin to flourish."

Since 1982, the nursing home has been owned by Hillhaven Corporation, one of the country's largest providers of rehabilitation and restorative care. The Gastonia Nursing Center's history goes back to 1967, when the Holiday Inn conglomerate built it as Medicenter of America at 416 N. Highland Street.

The first administrator was Charles Reid, who was followed by Bill Parker and Robert Neil. In 1971, the center was bought by Dr. Clyde Parker and William Phillipe, who changed the name to Gaston Nursing Center and oversaw the facility's conversion from a rehabilitation center to a more comprehensive nursing center.

Guardian Care bought the facility in 1978, and four years later sold it to the Hillhaven Corporation. Hillhaven traces its beginnings to 1946 in a single nursing home located in Olympia, Washington. It is now the second-largest operator of long-term care facilities in the country. The company owns, leases, or manages nursing centers and retirement housing communities throughout the nation. It's Medisave Pharmacy subsidiary operates retail and institutional pharmacies in the communities Hilllhaven serves

to better meet the needs of their residents.

Gastonia's Hillhaven Healthcare has a staff of 125, which includes the therapeutic staff, dietary, enrivonmental services, and the business office. It handles Medicare and Medicaid residents, as well as those with private funds or insurance. It also serves clients of Hospice of Gaston County. Hospice is a nonprofit organization that provides medical, social, psychological, and pastoral services to terminally ill persons and their families. Hillhaven Healthcare is proud to provide space and nursing staff for hospice patients. "It's a wonderful program providing a service to the community," says Admissions Coordinator Angie McDuffie.

Hillhaven offers many extras at its 25,000-square-foot facility in Gastonia: an in-house beauty shop, special therapeutic services, social services, activities, and dietary management. "Emphasizing one's abilities and encouraging residents to think positively and work toward their goals, one step at a time" is the credo of

Hillhaven Healthcare's employees.

Administrators since 1971 have included Sue B. Payne, Troy Hefner, Pete Moore, and Kathy Putnam. Bob Goon, the current administrator, assumed his position in 1994. Of note, Sue B. Payne went on to become a leader in the nursing home industry. She was president of the North Carolina Health Care Facilities Association and served on the licensing board for the appointment of administrators. Payne was also instrumental in the development of the Administrator in Training (AIT) program at the University of North Carolina-Chapel Hill.

Stressing that each resident is a whole person with many unique abilities and special needs, Hillhaven Healthcare's philosophy involves early treatment geared toward a goal of returning home or increasing independence in daily living skills and improved self-esteem.

Following in a tradition of caring, Hillhaven Healthcare of Gastonia remains committed in serving the community today and in the future generations to come.❏

Hillhaven offers many extras at its 25,000-square-foot facility in Gastonia.

AAA/Wide World Travel

The late Buren Shuford Neill, Jr. spent 30 years gathering the kinds of tips that his travel clients craved, whether it was where to book a hotel in Rio de Janiero or which sidewalk cafe to frequent in Paris.

He founded the first travel agency in Gastonia, now AAA/Wide World Travel Agency, Inc., a branch of the Carolina Motor Club based in Charlotte. Carolina Motor Club is part of the family of 131 AAA Clubs that serve some 35 million members.

Travel was far different when Neill started Wide World Travel Services, Inc. in 1956. Airline tickets were handwritten. If a trip included travel on several different airlines, a separate ticket was written for each leg of the trip. Records were kept on hundreds of three-by-five-inch index cards.

A native of Kings Mountain, Neill's background was in accounting. He attended Davidson College for a year, then was drafted into the Army and awarded two Purple Hearts for combat during World War II in Europe. Later he worked as comptroller for Neisler Mills, until the company was sold. Then he decided to go into business for himself, opening up an office at 218 East Franklin.

"He loved to travel. That was something he always wanted to do," remembers his son Buren Shuford (Chip) Neill III, now manager of travel support services for Carolina Motor Club in Charlotte.

At first, Buren Neill, Jr. ran the office with one other agent, Martha Caldwell. They booked mostly leisure trips.

The first corporate client was Textiles, Inc. and its subsidiary Threads USA. In the early 1960s, corporate business began growing rapidly, as air travel expanded throughout the United States. Today, corporate

The current office staff of **AAA/Wide World Travel.**

travel makes up 60 percent of AAA/Wide World Travel's business.

In the 1970s, international travel grew dramatically. Wide World Travel Services booked an around-the-world trip in 1970 for a group attending the Baptist World Alliance meeting in Tokyo. Neill accompanied the group, along with the rest of his family. The Foreign Mission Board, based in Richmond, Virginia, was a regular client. Missionaries from all over the world made travel arrangements through the agency.

Computers revolutionized the travel business over the next decade. Wide World Travel Services was the first computerized travel agency in Gastonia. In 1980, the company bought a system developed by ITT, Eastern Airlines, and Honeywell that gave them direct access to five airlines. Then Neill updated the technology in 1982 with a System One network, which allowed the agency to book directly with 488 airlines throughout the world.

After Neill suffered a heart attack in 1987, he decided to sell the company

to Ralph Peters, president of Carolina Motor Club. Joining the AAA network gave the agency access to a wide range of services. Chip Neill, who joined the company in 1978 after graduating from Carson Newman College, became general manager after the buy out. He moved to the corporate office in Charlotte in 1993, and Patti Black took over as manager in Gastonia. She has worked in the travel industry since 1978.

The Neill family has long been active in a wide range of civic activities. They are charter members of Charlotte's SKAL club, an international travel club for executives.❏

Homelite

*H*omelite's decision to build a plant in Gastonia in 1957 was significant to the area for two reasons: The company eventually provided hundreds of new jobs, and it gave the county a manufacturing plant outside of textiles, the dominant industry.

Homelite employs 1,200 workers who assemble a wide range of products, including generators, chain saws, multi-purpose saws, blowers, string trimmers, and edgers. The plant occupies a 550,000-square-foot facility near South U.S. Highway 321. Homelite manufactures and distributes its products on a worldwide basis and is the only company that makes outdoor power equipment solely in the United States.

The company underwent a modernization process between 1992 and 1994 that freed up space and cut down dramatically on materials handling. The new process cut material movement in half and freed up 65,000 square feet in space. It also allowed the company to increase warehouse capacity approximately 50 percent.

Such efficiency allows Homelite to produce in excess of 12,000 products a day, or about 30 trailer loads. The company has made other changes. A team of about nine workers, who are self-directed, assemble professional saws, a change from the traditional assembly-line system. The new process has improved quality and efficiency. Homelite involves employees in numerous committees to improve morale and efficiency. The company offers an in-house continuing education program that allows employees who are high school dropouts to earn their GED, the equivalent of a high school diploma.

The company chose Gastonia for its supply of skilled labor and access to

The "Class of 1957" includes nine (9) employees who started in 1957, the year **Homelite** *began operations in Gastonia.*

the Charlotte airport and interstate highways. It started with about 150 employees, nine of whom are still at the Gastonia facility. They are Morris Hall, Gene Steele, Gerald Buchanan, Joe Clemmer, Dean Deese, Lois Robinson, Jerry Miller, Bob Crunkelton, and Ernest McFalls.

The plant began making 25 to 50 power saws a day. It underwent expansions in 1967, 1972, and 1979. By the early 1970s, it employed more than 2,000 people. During the height of the 1970's energy crisis, Homelite built more than a million chain saws.

When Hurricane Hugo hit the Charlotte area in 1989, Homelite sold chain saws and generators from the backs of trucks as a service to area residents whose homes and businesses were damaged by the storm. Normally, all of its sales are through dealers and mass merchants such as

Wal-Mart and Home Depot.

Homelite got its start when inventor Charles H. Ferguson designed a small, lightweight gasoline-engine-driven generator in 1921. He named it Homelite since it was used to light homes in rural areas where regular electric power was not available. In 1975, Homelite moved its corporate headquarters from Port Chester, New York, to Carowinds Boulevard in Charlotte. The company also has plants in Greer and Columbia, South Carolina, and sales offices throughout the world.

David G. Walker has been general manager of the Gastonia operation since 1991. Employees are active in a wide range of civic activities, including the United Way and Red Cross. A number of employees are volunteer firefighters and emergency response technicians.❑

The **Homelite** *plant occupies a 550,000-square-foot facility near South U.S. Highway 321.*

*G*aston College

Since it was organized 30 years ago, Gaston College has grown into one of the largest community colleges in North Carolina with an unduplicated student headcount of approximately 25,000 annually.

The college has close ties to business and industry. Like other community colleges in the North Carolina system, its mission is to provide a broad array of programs aimed at helping students acquire specific skills, workforce preparedness, preparing students for a four-year university, or simply enriching their lives through continuing education.

All this started in 1965, when three institutions were combined to form

Gaston College. They were the Gaston Industrial Education Center, which taught vocational courses; Gaston Tech, which offered two-year associate degrees in engineering technology as an extension of N.C. State University; and Gaston College, which offered two-year liberal arts and business education degrees under the State Board of Higher Education. A county bond issue was passed to build the Craig Arts & Sciences classroom facility and the library science building.

Gaston College was named for a boarding school which operated from 1887 to 1905 in Dallas. The Wyss Information Center was modeled closely after the tower of the main

Gaston College has grown into one of the largest community colleges in North Carolina. Photo by Rick Haithcox.

building of the boarding school. The campus is now made up of 11 buildings and also includes a location in Lincolnton.

C. Grier Beam, founder of Carolina Freight Carriers Corp., was chairman of the Gaston County Board of Commissioners when Gaston College was created and, over the years, contributed more than $800,000 to the college in property, stock, and cash. He was a major contributor to the Beam Administration Building and the Lena Sue Beam Health Sciences Center.

Gaston College's programs are

diverse. The school offers three degree programs—associate of arts, associate of fine arts, and associate of science. Through these programs, Gaston College students may matriculate into universities. There are also one-year diploma programs and classes for certification in certain areas. Corporate and Community Education programs offer short courses for the general public, professional development for managers and professionals, and industrial training for the special needs of business and industry in Gaston and Lincoln counties. There is also a New and Expanding Industry Program that encourages businesses to create more jobs by providing funding for specialized training courses.

Other programs that fall under Corporate and Community Education include occupational extension courses, training and advice provided by the Small Business Center, and programs in criminal justice, emergency medical services, and fire science.

Basic study programs help high school dropouts, a cooperative education program designed to give students a chance to work while completing their degrees, and a number of programs utilizing television, radio, and cable to reach students in locations away from the main campus.

Gaston College is accredited by the Commission on Colleges of the Southern Association of Colleges and Schools. More than 20 other regional and national organizations accredit specific programs in the curriculum.❏

B.F. Goodrich

*T*he B.F. Goodrich plant on South U.S. Highway 321 has produced various polymers and additives for the textile industry since 1973.

The plant has undergone several transitions since it was founded by the late Maurice J. Walsh III, a Gastonia entrepreneur. Walsh was a native of Knoxville, Tennessee. He grew up in Gastonia and graduated from Belmont Abbey College in 1962 before starting his own company.

The business, first called Walsh Chemical Company, produces acrylic polymer latexes, styrene butadiene rubber (SBR) latexes and compounds used to increase the strength and wearability of carpet and fabrics in upholstery, drapery, mattresses and other products. Its chemicals are also used in adhesive, paint, and paper products.

State-of-the-art equipment is used to produce styrene butadiene rubber.

The plant occupies 23 acres of land on Telegraph Drive, just off South U.S. Highway 321. It has undergone several expansions. In 1980, the acrylic polymer plant was constructed to produce acrylic, vinyl acetate, acrylonitrile and other polymers as intermediates for the compound plant.

In 1985, Walsh Chemical Company was purchased by Interchem, the North American Division of RTZ Chemicals, based in the United Kingdom. RTZ Chemicals constructed the SBR polymer plant to produce latex for the textile coating, carpet, and paper industries.

Rhône-Poulenc, France's leading manufacturer of chemicals, purchased RTZ Chemicals in 1989, and the Gastonia plant became part of the Latex and Specialty Polymers Unit of the Specialty Chemicals Division. It was sold to B.F. Goodrich in 1994. B.F. Goodrich, based in Akron, Ohio, provides manufacturers with a wide range of specialty chemicals and products for the aerospace industry.

A total of 120 employees work at the Gastonia plant which has an annual payroll of more than $2.6 million. Johnny Ross joined as plant manager in 1992 after managing a plant in Dalton, Georgia. Larry McDaniel has been business manager for seven years.

The plant was nominated for Rhône-Poulenc's President's Safety Award in 1994 after achieving two years with no lost time accidents and completing 1993 without a recordable accident.

The company is active in a wide range of civic and community activities. It is a partner with H.H. Beam Elementary School, a supporter of the local volunteer fire departments, a member of the Environmental Affairs Committee for the Gastonia Chamber of Commerce, and a participant in the local downtown festival, Fish Camp Jam.❏

Quality control laboratory.

Polymer research and development laboratory.

Southwest Acoustical Specialties, Inc.

Dozens of new high-rise buildings and office park complexes began going up in the early 1970s. Lewis Carpenter, then a supervisor for a Charlotte company that installed acoustical walls and office partitions, saw an opportunity.

He left his job to start Southwest Acoustical Specialties Co., Inc., a company in Bessemer City that could provide the same services as his old employer on 24-hour notice. Much of the new space was speculative, and developers needed to custom finish office space as soon as it was leased.

Carpenter, who had been in the business since 1959, drove his truck all over the Piedmont scouting building projects and offering his services to anyone who looked like a potential customer.

He started out with a partner, the late L.P. Fletcher. They opened up shop in a tiny storage shed adjacent to a convenience store owned by Fletcher. They took calls through Fletcher's wife, who had a phone at her crafts store.

Since incorporating in 1976, Carpenter has overseen the company's growth into one of the largest acoustical contractors in the Southeast. Southwest Acoustical Specialties, Inc. does work for school systems, developers, contractors, architects, and building owners. Most of the work is within a 50-mile radius of Gastonia.

Southwest Acoustical Specialties employs 45 full time, and goes up to 77 employees during the summer, when extensive school work is done. The first employee Carpenter ever hired, William Bell, is still foreman, and 10 others have been with the company a decade or more. Executive Vice President Robert Jordan has been with the company 14 years.

Fletcher retired in 1977 for health reasons, and Carpenter bought his stock. The company netted $56,000 in profit during its first two years. An early client was Boston-based Spaulding and Sly Construction Co., which had a branch office at the Wachovia Center in Charlotte. Southwest Acoustical Specialties, Inc. upfitted 20 floors of the Wachovia Center on South Tryon.

Carpenter kept his building on East Virginia for just over a year before selling it and moving to a 5,000-square-foot building constructed on farmland he inherited from his father. He has expanded twice since then, adding a 3,000-square-foot office building and an 8,000-square-foot warehouse.

The company orders tractor-trailer loads of materials from U.S. Gypsum and Celotex, a division of Jim Walters Homes. Southwest Acoustical Specialties, Inc. expanded in the 1980s to do metal stud drywall work.

Carpenter got into the business after serving in the Air Force in the late 1950s. As a child, he picked cotton and drove a tractor. He got his first job in town at age fourteen, as a car hop.

"I was always mechanically inclined," says Carpenter. "I can remember when I was seven or eight years old taking Dad's Big Ben alarm clock apart to see what made it work."

When he left the service, a friend told him about a job at Acoustics, Inc.

Robert Jordan

Lewis Carpenter

in Charlotte. He began doing installations and became a supervisor in 1969.

But he knew he could do more on his own. "I saw a dire need for a service-oriented company that could perform work on a 24-hour notice."❑

Chambers Container Co. Inc.

Randy and Scott Chambers started their business in 1976 and continue to improve their products and efficiency.

Brothers Randy and Scott Chambers each headed different directions out of high school. Randy played defensive end for Duke University, graduated with a degree in zoology, and took a sales job with Amoco Chemical covering seven states from his base in Raleigh. Scott worked in manufacturing and started his own corrugated box factory in Gastonia.

When Randy tired of traveling, and Scott's partnership didn't work out, the two hooked up and formed Chambers Container, a corrugated box manufacturer that serves 600 customers, employs 56 people, and occupies a 54,000-square-foot building near South U.S. Highway 321.

Its service set the company apart. The Danaher Tool Group, which buys up to 1.5 million boxes a year from Chambers, recently gave the company its Extra Mile Award. The award recognizes suppliers that deliver products at a moment's notice when necessary and go to extraordinary measures to avoid cost increases.

"You delivered the product on short demand, often in a personal auto, to avoid a line shutdown," the company wrote in a letter of commendation.

Chambers buys flat corrugated sheets from its suppliers and processes them through machines that cut, print, fold, and glue the sheets to the customer's specifications. Turnaround time is 5 to 7 days—and sometimes faster.

"Anybody can get boxes delivered in two weeks. It's those unusual situations, where they call you and they need boxes right away, where you build loyalty," says Randy Chambers.

The brothers started their business in 1976 in 8,000 square feet of rented warehouse space in Ranlo. In the early days, Randy spent the day selling, and Scott ran the machines and made deliveries. After business hours, both worked in production, often late into the night. Sometimes they slept on cots in the back of the building.

Bryant Electric Supply was one of their first customers. "They've done things to help us cut costs. They were the first people who said, `Let us do you a favor—let us warehouse for you,'" says Harry Bryant, Jr. "I look at them like I look at us. We're a family

business. As time goes by, there are fewer and fewer of us. I'd rather do business with people locally. I feel they're going to look after your interests a little better."

The Chambers started their business by borrowing $50,000 to pay for overhead and buy a press and gluer, raw materials, and an old truck. After six months, they were making enough money to pay themselves $50 a week.

Now they have four modern, computerized machines and a fleet of three tractors and six trailors. The International Association of Independent Corrugated Converters recently awarded Chambers Containers second and third place in industrial design for their products. Randy Chambers, who serves on the board of the association, has also been recognized by the Gastonia Jaycees for community service and served as president of the Gaston Chamber of Commerce.

Chambers Container continues to work to improve its products and efficiency. It recently underwent an audit to be certified as a World Class Manufacturing Vendor by one of its customers, Vermont American. World Class Manufacturing is a system of benchmarking that industries use to eliminate waste and improve customer service.

At press time Chambers Container was closing on the aquisition of a similar type company that would double their current size when fully integrated into their operation. Also, they will close shortly on a partnership with several other box manufacturers to operate a plant that will produce the raw material that is used to manufacture boxes. Truly a company that is active and still growing.❏

Texlon Plastics

Texlon Plastics Corp. began in Tony Beam's garage in 1976 and has grown to be the area's largest manufacturer of plastic injection molded industrial products.

The company has undergone four major expansions since it was founded and now occupies a 23,400-square-foot facility near South U.S. Highway 321 in Gastonia.

Although about half of its sales are to the textiles industry, Texlon also supplies plastic parts for a wide range of other manufacturers. It produces keypads for computers, plastic boards on which electronic parts are mounted for telephone equipment, and components for the automotive industry.

Texlon did $3.2 million in sales in 1993, up 22 percent over 1992 and typical of its steady growth over the past 18 years.

Founder Tony Beam started the company in his 800-square-foot garage in 1976. By that time, he had 15 years of experience in manufacturing and sales. A high school dropout, Beam took his first full-time job at age 17 as a parts manager for a machine assembly plant in Bessemer City. He took a demotion to move to another machine shop as stock boy, knowing that he would have the opportunity to move up to the position of salesman.

The textile industry was just beginning to discover the potential of plastic machine parts. Beam scrambled to find the parts his customers wanted and became acquainted with Hope Plastics in Bessemer City.

Owner Bill Hope had just two employees, but he saw that Beam was a good salesman and knew the business was growing. He hired Beam away, and in his first year with Hope Plastics, Beam doubled sales. He was eventually made vice president of manufacturing.

"I came up with some pretty good designs," Beam says. "Making the customer's machinery work better made me look good."

Beam stayed with Hope Plastics for eight years. He decided that, because it was a family-owned business, his future was limited, and it was time to strike out on his own. He parted amiably with Bill Hope, borrowed $10,000 on his house and accepted a $3,000 investment from his father, a textile machine fixer.

He ran a couple of 30-year-old, reconditioned machines at night in his garage, sold during the day, and slept a few hours in the afternoon, when his father would run the machines. After eight months, he took on partner

William R. Glover, an experienced machinist and mold maker who worked for Plastic Products in King Mountain. Now vice president and head of Texlon's tool and die and molding departments, Glover has been instrumental in helping orchestrate the company's growth. It employs 47 people.

The company's main market is the Southeast, but it does about 5 percent of its sales in Europe, Latin America, Canada, and India.

"We've tried to have controlled growth," says Beam. "We try not to take any more business than we can handle."

The company works with 30 distributors who buy parts for the textile industry. But Beam still personally calls on local accounts such as Pharr Yarns and Parkdale Mills. He also attends a half-dozen trade shows every year to sell to other industries.

The company continues to grow, planning a 10,000-square-foot addition in 1994. Beam oversees sales and management, and Glover concentrates on manufacturing.

"We think alike," says Beam. "We're both hard workers."❑

President Tony Beam

Vice President William R. Glover

Home Health Care Of Gaston Co., Inc.

Home Health Care of Gaston County, Inc. is available 24 hours a day, 7 days a week.

Celebrating 15 years of service to our community

When Eileen Klimkowski, RN, went back to school in the 1970s to receive her BSN, little did she realize that during her course of study an idea would be born that would, 15 years later, provide over 100 jobs for members of the community, as well as provide a much needed service to Gaston and adjacent counties.

Klimkowski began her nursing career as a navy nurse. "The Navy gave me a lot of management experience," she says. After seven years of service, she opted for marriage and raised four children.

While attending the University of North Carolina at Charlotte (UNCC), she was asked to follow a patient home from the hospital. Her patient was an elderly retired nurse who had suffered complications from diabetes. By providing home care, Klimkowski was able to improve the woman's quality of life and hospital re-admissions were decreased. "I was able to make a difference," Klimkowski remembers.

In 1979, Klimkowski received her BSN and established Home Health Care of Gaston County, Inc. (HHC of GC). HHC of GC was Gaston County's first private home health care. Initially operating out of Klimkowski's home, the first year she and a part-time staff of 15 served 83 clients making a total of 1,040 visits. Currently, there are 108 clinical and administrative employees responsible for the care of over 1,000 clients each year.

In 1992, HHC of GC was able to build their own office and moved into their current location at 2923 Rousseau Court, Gastonia.

Louise Glenn called in HHC of GC to help care for her terminally ill husband. "I could never have done it without them," she says. "My husband loved the nurses. He could be home with his family."

A firm believer in higher education, Klimkowski received her Masters in Community Health Administration at the University of South Carolina. She also works with the nursing program at UNCC to provide their student nurses a rotation of home health experience.

Home Health Care of Gaston County, Inc. received CHAP Accreditation (Community Health Accreditation Program—a subsidiary of the National League for Nursing) in March of 1994.

Home Health Care of Gaston County, Inc. is available 24 hours a day, 7 days a week for short and long term care of post-hospital clients, infants, and homebound individuals with physical and medical conditions. Certified and licensed, this agency offers nursing, maternal/infant care, personal care, medical social work, respiratory, nutrition, physical, speech, and occupational therapies.

"Eileen has a high level of commitment to quality, which comes across in her dedication to meet the needs of the community with the best staff and equipment she can round up," states Jim McKenzie, Chairman of HHC of GC's Professional Advisory Committee (PAC). The PAC meets quarterly to help Home Health Care identify healthcare needs in Gaston County.❑

"Service is the heart of our business."

Tender loving care at home.

Beverly Knits

Very few knitting companies had the technology to knit specialty fabrics when Beverly Knits opened in 1980. A new stretch fabric containing spandex was gaining popularity. Beverly Knits was one of the first manufacturers to successfully knit the spandex fabric.

Founded by Robert and Jo Ann Sytz, the company found a special niche in the textile market. Beverly Knits soon became known for its ability to work with difficult specialty fabrics. It's more exciting to be doing something that's new and different, even though difficult," says Bob Sytz, Sr.

The company became known as a family business when two sons and a daughter joined the business. Ron, vice president of manufacturing joined in 1983; Beverly, personnel manager for whom the company was named, joined in 1987; and Bob, Jr. controller, joined in 1991.

The company outgrew the 8,000 square feet of leased space and eight knitting machines with which it started in Bessemer City. Beverly Knits now occupies a 100,000-square-foot plant in West Gastonia that has undergone several additions since it was built in 1987. Another 11,000-square-foot addition is planned by 1996. The company operates 96 single- and double-knit machines. When the facility was built in 1987, Beverly Knits had 80 employees. Now the company has 150 employees.

The company's growth has reflected changes in the apparel industry. The active wear market exploded in the late 1980s, using spandex in fabric to give it the "stretch and recovery" properties that make sports clothes a comfortable fit. Only about 20 percent of the country's knitters have the capability to knit spandex. Beverly Knits serves other niche markets, as well.

They can knit fiberglass into fabric used for fireproofing mattresses and upholstery. They can also plate spandex with two yarns, such as cotton and nylon, for fabric used in intimate apparel.

Beverly Knits is an outstanding technical knitter," says Steve Wald, president of Naturally Knits, Inc. in Winston-Salem. "They're very inventive in defining new knit constructions. They re-invest very heavily in their business, which means they have a wide array of the latest generations of machinery."

Operating a fast-growing company that specializes in knitting high tech fabrics requires a well-trained work force. "You can have all the new equipment and new facilities you want, but it's people who make the company successful," says Bob Sytz, Sr. Beverly Knits has instituted several programs aimed at retaining good employees.

Besides offering competitive wages and a 401K profit sharing plan, the company gives bonuses for good attendance. A "Bring a Friend to Work" campaign encourages employees to act as recruiters for the company. The company also offers classes in first-aid, cardio-pulmonary resuscitation and smoking cessation.

Employees are encouraged to be active in a wide range of community activities. The company received a Golden Eagle Award in 1993 for being a top supporter of the Gaston United Way. Mr. Sytz is president-elect of the Rotary Club of Gastonia. Ron Sytz is chairmen of the 1994 Fish Camp Jam celebration in Gastonia. Beverly is active in the Gaston County Personnel Association and chairman of the Textile Week Committee. Bob, Jr. serves on the Executive Committee of the Gaston Manufacturers Health Care Coalition.

Bob Sytz, Sr. grew up in the textile business. He worked in his father's knitting operation in Dyersburg, Tennessee, and earned a degree in textile engineering from Georgia Tech. After graduating, he worked for Malden Mills in Lawrence, Massachusetts, as manager of the finishing department, and as director of research and development for Armtex, Inc. in Pilot Mountain, North Carolina, before starting Adventure Knits, Inc. with other investors in the 1970s. When Adventure Knits was sold, he started Beverly Knits.

A family business requires a special commitment, says Mr. Sytz. "You're not only father and son and daughter and mother, but you're managers working together."❏

The company became known as a family business when two sons and a daughter joined the business. (L to R) Ron, Jo Ann, Beverly, Bob Sr., Bob, Jr.

Conitex

Conitex Headquarters in Gaston, NC
Shown above is the combined administrative and production headquarters for Conitex, a 10-year-old company that has become a leader in providing paper cone technology for the textile yarn industry.

*T*he product looks simple: It's a cone used to hold yarn during manufacturing. But as simple as it appears, Conitex has found ways to improve it. In little over a decade, the Conitex plant in Gastonia has established a new standard in paper cones, introduced innovations, and captured 40 percent of the U.S. market.

Conitex was founded by Joseph Artiga, a Spaniard whose family has been in the cone business since the turn of the century. The company, part of Miami-based Texmaco USA, Inc., opened its Gastonia plant in 1982, just as the textile industry began extensive modernization. New, increasingly automated machinery required greater precision in the components of manufacturing.

Conitex met the challenge. The cones, which carry yarn, are placed by robot on winders. They must be a precise fit on the winders to work. Conitex produces cones that are within a millimeter of specifications.

"Dimensional accuracy and tolerance have been keys in product acceptance," says General Manager Michael Schmidlin.

There are other features that Conitex has introduced. Conitex cones have a plush surface that allows the yarn to adhere better and more consistently, which is important in the knitting and weaving processes. The company also introduced printing on the tip and base of the cones. This is a color band or design that signifies a certain yarn type and helps manufacturers and their clients in inventory and production tracking.

Engineers work closely with textile equipment manufacturers to develop new cones for new equipment. Nothing is wasted; the cones are made from recycled newspapers and later can be recycled themselves.

Conitex has a turnaround time of two weeks and is able to serve some customers with just a week's lead time.

"Our relationship on delivery, service, and quality of product has been excellent," says Donnie Hitt, corporate purchasing manager at China Grove Textiles, Inc., which buys more than five and a half million cones a year from Conitex.

Conitex serves 100 clients, with half of the market in North Carolina and the rest mostly in the Southeast. Some clients are also in California and the Northeast. Exports make up about 5 percent of sales.

Besides supplying the textile industry, the company also found a niche market in megaphones used for sporting events. It trademarked the name "Megacone" and sells specially made cones imprinted with the names of sports teams. Customers have included the NBA's Utah Jazz and North Carolina high schools.

The company continues to grow and is currently undergoing its third expansion, which will give it a total of 105,000 square feet, more than four times its original size. Seventy-five people work at the Gastonia plant.

Conitex is also a strong supporter of the community. In 1993, the company received the Bronze Gold Eagle Award for its high level of participation in the Gaston County United Way fund-raising campaign.

Schmidlin has been with the company since 1985, except for a hiatus in 1988-1989, when he started the company's Taiwan operation. Conitex, which also has plants in Spain and England, opened up a fifth plant in Indonesia in 1993.

"We have a very clear understanding of what the market wants and needs," says Schmidlin. "We are able to quickly translate that into concrete advantages through our engineering division."❏

The Business Is Cones
Conitex executives (left to right), Director of Development, David Monteith; General Manager, Michael Schmidlin; & Sales Director & Corporate Secretary, Leary Cloer are shown at their Gastonia, NC, headquarters, confering on new developments in their product line.

Countrytime Rest Home

In the summer of 1980, Gloria McDonald tuned into a television special entitled "What are we going to do with Mother?" The program, which dealt with the concerns of a family facing long term placement for a loved one, caused her to realize the need for personal quality care. She had some experience with caring for older relatives and found it most rewarding. She envisioned building a facility to provide the best care possible in a home-type atmosphere.

She talked with her sister, Linda Eckard, who caught her enthusiasm and together they began making plans, even though neither had any experience in the rest home field. All they had was a dream and conviction they were doing the right thing.

Today Mrs. McDonald oversees a pleasant, airy, facility called Countrytime. The home has 62 beds and a staff of 44 employees. Several living rooms and the dining areas are named for former residents, whose portraits are displayed as treasured memories.

Gloria, a former secretary, built the facility on a piece of land she and husband, Wilson, owned near Crowders Mountain. She had the land and Linda cashed in $16,000 saved up in retirement from her job at Burlington Mills. A local bank gave them a loan and H.S. Poole, a retired contractor, supervised the project and acted as a mentor, helping them with additional funds to complete construction. Both Gloria and Linda worked along with Mr. Poole's crew, clearing the property, insulating walls, painting, and etc.

On April 2, 1982 the vision became reality when the 20 bed home was opened. Avery Carpenter of Gastonia was the first resident; then came four more, and soon the beds were filled.

The sisters did most of the work, along with Patsy Blake, the dietician whose employment continues still with excellent food service. Within two years, Countrytime had 12 employees, 20 residents, and an annual payroll of $75,000.

Since then, Mrs. McDonald has overseen two additions. Countrytime now has 50 residents. "Let's not mention payroll now," says Gloria. "I've always been told I have too many employees. I have double the staff the state requires; but, I'm confident our residents get a lot of personal attention and are well cared for."

Countrytime is licensed as a domiciliary facility, a home for relatively healthy elderly adults. However, they continue to care for residents whose health declines, as long as the family and physician are pleased with the care. This policy began with a resident named Minnie Queen whose health deteriorated while at Countrytime. She was moved to another facility, but the family was unhappy with the situation. When they met Mrs. McDonald several weeks later in downtown Gastonia, they told her their feelings. With some adjustments, Mrs. Queen was moved back and she stayed until her death five years later. Her portrait hangs in the "Minnie Queen Parlor." "They were just like my family," says Minnie's daughter, Shirley Ferguson. "My mother would not have lived as long as she did without their good care."

Linda Eckard served as co-administrator until 1986, when she and husband, Buddy, parted amicably and sold their interest to the McDonalds. Another sister, Carolyn Whitworth, has worked as supervisor since 1987. Christie Cooke of Kings Mountain now serves as co-administrator.

"I really enjoy my work," says Mrs. McDonald. "We build a good relationship with our families; for when you meet the needs of their loved ones, a bond is developed between you that is lasting."❑

Wilson & Gloria McDonald

Avery Carpenter is served by Rachael Gantt.

Black & Whisnant Properties, Inc.

Black & Whisnant Properties, Inc. began at Thelma Whisnant's kitchen table, where she and partner Doug Black organized their business and decided to strike out on their own in 1983.

Their goal was to have at least 50 residential listings within six months. Within two years, they were listing an average of 40 houses a month.

Today, they oversee 13 other independent agents from their office at 2211 Union Road. Both are leaders in the real estate industry. Whisnant was president of the Gaston Board of Realtors in 1987, and named Realtor of the Year in 1985. Black was president of the Gaston County Multiple Listing Service in 1984.

The company started in a small office further down Union Road, where the partners rented a house. Within six months, Joe Yarborough approached the two about buying his house, which was being zoned for office use. He offered to finance the deal.

Since then, Black and Whisnant have done two additions, giving their office a total of 3,000 square feet. They started with one other agent and a secretary, and within five years had seven agents.

Both entered real estate by chance. Whisnant, a graduate of Ashley High School, worked 15 years as a machine threader for knitting machines at Pama Manufacturing. Both her parents had been textile mill workers.

She noticed a newspaper ad for courses at Gaston College, and decided to enroll. She quickly realized she couldn't work third shift at Pama and have time to study. About that time, she was offered a job as a receptionist at Harrison Realty. She worked full time while going to school and stayed at Harrison for a year after getting her license. Then she moved to Look Realty.

There she met Black, who had married after graduating from Hunter Huss College and worked as a furniture mover briefly. His father talked him into taking real estate courses, and he earned his license and worked for Eastridge Homes and then Look.

"My nature is that I'm a workaholic," says Black. "I found I could make money and apply myself and be rewarded."

When another Realtor® at Look announced she was leaving to work for a builder, Black and Whisnant began to think about leaving also and starting their own business. Others

told them they were crazy to locate on Union Road, two and a half miles from all the real estate companies on Garrison Boulevard. But growth has occurred in the southeast part of town where their office is located. It proved to be a good decision.

In 1991, Black & Whisnant became a franchise of Better Homes and Gardens. The new affiliation gave them national status and access to training and supplies. But they still think of themselves as a local company.

"Doug and I were both born here. Our roots are here," says Whisnant. "I want to improve Gaston County for my family. Even though we bought a franchise, Gaston County is our home."

Whisnant is a 1983 graduate of the Realtors Institute, and she is a Certified Real Estate Specialist (CRS). She is active in the Evening Optimists Club.

"Regardless of what you sell, you're dealing with a family," says Whisnant. "It's one of the biggest things they'll ever do. It's the same thing with selling. They're selling the biggest thing they've got. They're entrusting their life savings with us."❏

*Sales Staff of **Black & Whisnant Properties, Inc. Better Homes and Gardens**®*

Compleat Rehab & Sports Therapy Center

Cheryl Grant did a market survey in 1987 to determine the need for outpatient physical therapy services in Gastonia. She and partner Linda Grimsley decided there was enough interest to open a small practice.

They leased 1,100 square feet in a shopping center on Pembroke Road and outgrew it within six months. After a few years and several more expansions, they decided to look for land and begin planning their own 19,000-square-foot building.

"I had no idea we would be embraced by the community as well as we have been or grow as fast as we have," says Grant.

Compleat Rehab was the first outpatient rehabilitation center in Gastonia, other than services offered at Gaston Memorial Hospital.

Grant traveled around the state looking at other facilities before planning her own. The result is a contemporary, two-story building with light, airy rooms, an aquatic area with a therapeutic pool, and a "work hardening" center where workers recovering from injuries learn to do their jobs safely. A full kitchen allows occupational therapists to teach independent living skills. A splint fabrication center fashions specialty orthotic devices.

The business started with physical therapy services and within two years added speech and occupational therapy. It has two divisions: outpatient services, which handles about 20,000 patient visits a year; and contract services, which contracts with home health care agencies and state facilities to handle more than 40,000 patient visits a year.

Compleat Rehab employs 56, about two-thirds of them therapists or therapy assistants. The physical and occupational therapists have an average of more than 12 years' experience.

The company's "work hardening" program is housed in 3,000 square feet that resembles a factory workplace. Each patient's program is individualized. They learn how to lift, bend, stretch, or do other motions similar to those in their work routine. The program is aimed at helping injured workers recover completely.

The therapeutic pool helps patients recovery quickly.

"Statistically, if an injured worker is out of the work force more than six months, there's just a 50 percent chance that worker will return. If he or she is out of the workforce a year or more, the chance drops to zero," says Grant.

Although Grant's first love was physical therapy, she also has a background in business and management. A high school dropout, she worked odd jobs and decided to finish her high school equivalency at age 21 and go back to school. She earned a bachelor's in physical therapy at the University of Alabama and went to work for a national physical therapy group, Physical Therapy Associates. She rose quickly through the ranks to vice president and member of the board of directors, but decided she wanted something different from corporate life.

"If you're delivering a product, larger is better. But if you're delivering a service, larger is not necessarily better," says Grant. After earning an MBA from the University of Houston, she put together a small company in Charlotte that merged with a Tennessee based corporation. "All of a sudden I found myself back in that corporate structure," she recalls. That's when she decided to sell her interest and start a business in Gastonia.

"Having a locally owned business allows her to keep rates lower and focus on delivering services efficiently," says Grant.

"As a therapist, you have a dramatic effect on someone's life and a close relationship you can't have in other areas of medicine," says Grant. "No one should have to leave this community to go to Charlotte for these kinds of services."❏

Compleat Rehab *was the first outpatient rehabilitation center in Gastonia.*

China Grove Textiles, Inc.

Arlington Plant

China Grove Textiles, Inc. combined the best of two worlds when it was purchased in 1988 by the Japanese firm Kondo Cotton Spinning Co, Ltd. of Nagoya, Japan .

The Gastonia-based yarn spinning company has undergone extensive modernization and instituted numerous programs aimed at upgrading employees' skills.

The changes have improved efficiency and reduced downtime. China Grove's five plants produce 850,000 pounds of cotton yarns and polyester-blend yarns per week.

"We have combined the talents of both Japanese and American management," says Chief Executive Officer Don Warren, a native of Alabama who has worked in the textile industry since he was 16. "That gives us an advantage other companies don't have."

The new China Grove Textiles, Inc. replaced 80 percent of its equipment with high-tech machinery. It did away with incentive pay, a century-old tradition in the textile industry, in order to put more emphasis on quality. Management was trimmed from six to four layers.

Turnover has decreased by 300 percent under the new management. "That's important," says Warren, "because the increasingly automated textile industry relies on well-trained workers." CGT sells yarn to knitting and weaving operations with high-speed equipment. This means the yarn must be consistent in evenness and uniformity.

China Grove Textiles, Inc. also puts an emphasis on safety and environmental concerns. It recently received an environmental excellence award from the American Textile Manufacturers Institute. CGT recycles half of its solid waste, made up of dust particles from cotton plants, into feed for dairy and beef cattle. ATMI also recognized China Grove Textiles, Inc. as one of the original recipients of the Quest for the Best in Safety and Health Award.

"Customers recognize the emphasis on quality," says Warren. "There are a lot of good yarn manufacturers in America today. How do you set yourself apart? There's no one thing. It's a combination of capital expenditures and employee training and development."

In an effort to attract the best employees, the company beefed up its benefits package. An employee wellness program includes screening for medical conditions, special rates for employees at the YMCA, quarterly smoking cessation programs, and an emphasis on prenatal care. China Grove Textiles, Inc. added other benefits as well. It offered a credit union, tripled life-insurance benefits, increased accident and sickness pay by 25 percent, and adopted a 401(k) plan. The company also involves employees in supporting the United Way and other nonprofit organizations.

While the new China Grove Textiles, Inc. began in 1988, its mills have been in operation for more than half a century. The Kondo family acquired, from Dixie Yarns, the plants which make up China Grove Textiles, Inc. The plants were part of two older companies which Dixie Yarns bought in the 1980s. China Grove Cotton Mills, Inc. was established in 1922 in Rowan County. The Arlington and Mutual plants were part of Ti-Caro, Inc., which began in 1931 in Gaston County.

"We appreciate the past and our history, but China Grove Textiles, Inc. has been launched into the 21st century," says Warren. "The best yarn we're ever going to make will be tomorrow."❏

Mutual Plant

Patrons

*T*he following individuals, companies, and organizations have made a valuable commitment to the quality of this publication. Community Communications and the Gaston Chamber of Commerce gratefully acknowledge their participation in *Gaston Remembers: Weaving a Tapestry in Time.*

American Linc Corporation

Arnold Food Company

Beltex Corporation

CR Industries—Gastonia

Caldwell Home Care Services/Caldwell Drug Store

Carolina Electric Motor Services

City Club of Gastonia, Inc.

Collis and Associates

Fleischmann's Yeast, Inc.

Gaston Anesthesia Associates, P.A.

Gaston County Economic Development Commission

Gaston Radiology, I.A.

Gaston Women's Healthcare, P.A., Kelvin C. Harris, M.D.

Herman Reeves Sheet Metal

Landmasters, Inc.

Litchfield Fabrics of North Carolina

Machine Devices, Inc.

Moss Rexall Drugs, Inc.

Mount Holly Spinning, Division of Spray Cotton Mills

O.G. Penegar Company, Inc.

Petty Machine Company, Inc.

Precision Machine Products

Sherrill Industries, Inc.

Spencer-Pettus Machine Company, Inc.

Stewart Cooper Architects

Value Systems, Inc.

*P*hoto Acknowledgements

Over 700 old photographs have been collected in order to make the selections within this book. To those people that so graciously lent their photographs, we thank you very much. To those whose photographs were not able to be included, we thank you even more. Jim Brown, Jr.

American Efird Mills, Inc.

American Legion, Post #23, Gastonia

Mrs. R.B. Babington, Jr. (Helen Howe)

Bessemer City Record

Dennis Jane Black

Ray N. Blackwood

Carol Brackett

Jim Brown, Jr. (Cam-Art)

Bryant Electric Supply, Inc.

Mike Bush and Daniel Stowe Botanical Gardens Studio

City of Mt. Holly, Archives Department

Colonial America Re-enactment Group

Mrs. George Cramer and Family

Mary C. Crooke

The Dixie News

Dixie Yarns, Inc.

John Domhlo

49th Re-enactment Group of N.C.

Gaston County Art and History Museum

Gaston Chamber of Commerce

Gaston County School System

Gaston County Staff

Gaston Gazette

Gaston Health Care

Gastonia City Fire Department

Gastonia City Police Department

E.E. Goforth

Thelma and Fred Goodson

Charles D. Gray III and Family

Fred Gray

Jim Heracklis

Chip Holton

Fred and Creola Houser

Kermit Hull Photography

Scott Lewis

A.C. Lineberger III and Family

Long Creek Presbyterian Church

Wilma Long

Paul Mauney

Marshall McClure

McCord Aero Service

Freida Lankford Moses

Kay K. Moss

New Hope Presbyterian Church

Robert "Ezra" Nolen

North Carolina Department of Archives and History

Observer Printing Co.

Olney Presbyterian Church

Lucy R. Penegar

Pharr Yarns, Inc.

Bill Phillips

Pisgah A.R.P. Church

Jim Poag

Albert Rhyne

The Rhyne Family

Rick Haithcox Photography

Schiele Museum of Natural History

Shelby Studio

Therman Short

Ellen Holland Shuford

Lois Smith

Southern Textile Bulletin

Mrs. Thomas Worthy Springs, Jr. and Family

John Caleb Steele

Campbell Stewart

St. Marks Episcopal Church

Howell Stroup, Cherryville Historical Society

Harold T. Sumner

The Belmont Banner (Williams)

United States Department of Interior

Tom Watson and Jennie Craig Watson

Charles A. Wetzell

Basil L. Whitener Family

For the convenience of our readers that would like to obtain copies of photographs within this book: please note the number at the end of each photo caption. This number is on file with Jim Brown, Jr. at Cam-Art Studio in Gastonia, N.C.

$\mathcal{B}$ibliography

Blythe, Legette, *Robert Lee Stowe: Pioneer in Textiles*. Belmont, N.C. 1965.

Davenport, Douglas. "A History of Linwood College." Unpublished thesis, Appalachian State Teachers College, 1959.

"The Floods of July 1916." Southern Railway Company. 1917.

Gaston County Historical Bulletin, Gastonia, N.C.: Gaston County Historical Association.

The Gastonia Gazette, Gastonia, N.C.: Freedom Newspapers, Inc.

Gray, Charles. Interview, April, 1978.

Hoffman, Miles, *Our Kin.* Gastonia, N.C.: Gaston Historical Society.

Parder, J.T., and C.F. Park, Jr. "Gold Deposits of the Southern Piedmont." U.S. Geological Survey Professional Paper, 1948.

Pope, Liston, *Millhands and Preachers*. New Haven, Conn.: Yale University Press, 1942.

Puett, Minnie Stowe, *History of Gaston County*. Charlotte, N.C.: Observer Printing, 1939.

Reagan, Robert Allison. "Gaston County Textile Pioneers." Collection of papers in Gaston County Public Library.

Rhyne, Henry H. Interview, July, 1979.

Roberts, Bruce, *The Carolina Gold Rush* . Charlotte: McNally and Loftin, 1971.

Separk, Joseph H., "Gastonia and Gaston County, N.C.: Past, Present, and Future." Gastonia, N.C.: Joseph H. Separk, 1949.

Shuford, Ellen White Holland. Personal interview, November, 1993.

Stroupe, Howell. Personal interview. January, 1994.

Toney, Elaine White. Personal interview. October, 1993.

Williams, Dameron, ed. *Shiloh and Beyond: A History of the First Methodist Church, Gastonia, N.C. 1870-1970*. Gastonia, N.C.: 1970.

Williams, Robert L., *Gaston County: A Pictorial History*. Norfolk, Va.: Donning Company, 1981.

Gaston's Enterprises Index

ndex

Gaston Remembers

This book was typeset in Palatino and Snell Roundhand at Community Communications, Montgomery, Alabama and printed at Delmar Printing & Publishing, Charlotte, North Carolina.